Secondary Education in China after Mao:
Reform and Social Conflict

Stig Thøgersen

Secondary Education in China after Mao: Reform and Social Conflict

AARHUS UNIVERSITY PRESS

Copyright: Aarhus University Press, 1990
Word-processed by the author
Printed in Denmark by Aka-Print, Aarhus
ISBN 87 7288 219 0

AARHUS UNIVERSITY PRESS
Aarhus University, building 170
DK-8000 Aarhus C, Denmark

Contents

List of Tables

Acknowledgments

The idea of writing this book emerged in early 1984 while I was studying at the Education Department of Beijing Normal University. I am indebted to prof. Cheng Youxin, my supervisor at Beishida, and to Hu Xiaolu, Shi Jinghuan and other friends at the department for their help.

Other Chinese friends and colleagues, too many to mention by name, have helped me during my stays in China. My special appreciation goes to the Educational Bureaus of Yantai District and Harbin City for their hospitality and open-minded attitude.

The late Jesper Florander, director of the Danish Institute of Educational Research, provided valuable guidance and encouragement during the first stages of the project, and Gustav Leunbach of the same institution was a great help in the treatment and interpretation of the data from the Yantai survey.

I have also benefitted greatly from the instructive comments of Børge Bakken, Marianne Bastid, Anita Chan, Søren Clausen, Jørgen Delman, Greg Kulander, Steinar Kvale, Liu Yu-an, Matthias Risler and Jonathan Unger on parts or all of the manuscript at successive stages.

The Institute of East Asian Studies, University of Aarhus, has provided an inspiring base for my work, and I am grateful to Ivy Mortensen for her secretarial assistance. Special thanks to Greg Kulander for trying to make my English comprehensible.

Finally, I am indebted to the Danish Social Science Research Council and the Research Foundation of the University of Aarhus for financial support.

Aarhus,
January 1990

Stig Thøgersen

1. Introduction

Background and Content

This study will review and analyze the dramatic changes in Chinese secondary education in the period from the death of Mao Zedong and the subsequent overthrow of the remaining Cultural Revolution leaders in 1976 up to the crushing of the pro-democracy student movement in 1989. These changes deserve attention because they have deeply influenced the lives and careers of millions of young Chinese and because they reflect important general trends in China's political and social development through more than a decade of sweeping reforms in all fields.

Throughout the history of the People's Republic of China (PRC), education has been a hotly debated issue and educational policies have been subject to frequent changes and reversals. After 1976, the field of education was again one of the very first to be reformed in accordance with the visions of the new leaders, this time Deng Xiaoping and the reform wing of the Chinese Communist Party (CCP).

No part of China's educational system has undergone more deep-going reforms since 1976 than secondary education. First of all, the direct connection between middle school performance and career opportunities that existed before the Cultural Revolution has been reestablished through the introduction of an elaborate system of selective examinations and tests. Furthermore, vocational education has been strongly promoted, so that the different types of vocational schools which played only a minor role during the Cultural Revolution decade enrolled in 1988 45% of all students at senior middle school level. Finally, China has shifted its focus of attention from the "popularization" of education (*puji*) to the "raising of standards" (*tigao*). In practical terms this has meant that fewer students have been enrolled, particularly in senior middle school, while the period of schooling has been extended and the curriculum made more standardized, theory-oriented and academic. Secondary education has thus undergone a fundamental transformation over the past thirteen years.

It is the aim of the present study to review, analyze and discuss this transformation process and its results. In the course of the review, some officially propagated myths about Chinese education in the reform period will be reassessed. First of all, it has been, against the sinister background of the dogmatism, political indoctrination and widespread incompetence in Cultural

Revolution education, a comparatively easy task for the CCP to make the post-1976 educational reforms appear as a successful rescue operation, bringing Chinese schools back on their feet. However, as the present study will show, Chinese secondary education is still in a state of continuing crisis, a crisis which is particularly acute in the rural areas. Another officially promoted myth is that the reforms represent necessary readjustments of the educational sector to the objective demands of a society under modernization. A closer examination of the reforms, however, shows that they cannot possibly be explained as pure, value-free adaptions of education to economic realities. Factors like Chinese educational traditions, the ideology and historical trauma of the reformers as well as their need for support from the educated strata of society have strongly influenced the formulation and implementation of reform policies in secondary education. Finally, the study also shows that the rationality of the reforms has been further undermined by the internal dynamics of the reform process itself: in some cases control over the reforms has been lost, causing "side-effects" which have overshadowed the original purpose.

For students and researchers of contemporary China, this book will serve as a case study of the effects of the reform strategy in one important sector of Chinese society. Students of comparative education will hopefully find the book useful as an example of the problems confronting educational reforms in a Third World country where education has always been an extremely important method of achieving social status, and where educational policies are therefore constantly subject to intense public attention. The dilemmas that education in China has been facing (general vs. vocational, popularization vs. raising of standards, etc...) are universal, and the consequences of the fundamental changes in Chinese policies towards these questions therefore deserve international attention.

A number of excellent books have been written on China's experiences in the educational field in the period from the victory of the revolution in 1949 up to the introduction of the post-Mao reforms. In my eyes, the most interesting works have been those that combine an account of educational policies with a socio-logical analysis of their effects upon students, parents and teachers. Susan L. Shirk's *Competitive Comrades* and Jonathan Unger's *Education Under Mao* are model examples of such works focusing on the period before 1976.[1] Various aspects of the post-Mao reforms in secondary education have been dealt with in works by Western scholars such as Stanley Rosen, Suzanne Pepper, Matthias

---

1. *Shirk 1982, Unger 1982.*

Risler and several others.[2] Today, however, where the reforms have had more than a decade to prove their worth, I believe that a coherent review covering all the major aspects of the reforms as well as their social effects will be a timely addition to this literature.

I have based the study not only on Chinese documents and reports, but also on materials collected through five months of field research in China during three periods in 1984, 1986 and 1987. I followed classes in a middle school for a week, visited different types of secondary schools, conducted a questionnaire survey and had formal as well as informal interviews with many middle school students and teachers.

The book is organized as follows: *Chapters 2 to 4* provide the general background for discussing the reforms carried out in secondary education by presenting the historical, political and social context in which the reforms have been implemented. *Chapter 2* is a historical overview of secondary education in China with special emphasis on the experiences with different educational "models". *Chapter 3* examines how the general political and ideological climate of the reform decade put narrow constraints on the educational reforms. *Chapter 4* describes how formal education during the reform period became much more vital for upward social mobility, thus increasing the social value of gaining access to high quality middle schools.

Chapter 5 opens the discussion of the main topic with a general presentation of the structure, aims, curriculum and funding of secondary education in China. *Chapter 6* examines the quantitative results of the reforms and shows that a smaller proportion of the relevant age group received secondary education in 1988 than in the 1970s and that the problem of students dropping out of school was very serious all through the reform period. *Chapter 7* looks at the reintroduction of the examination system, the establishment of elite ("key") schools, the streaming of students into "fast" and "slow" classes and at the shock effect generated as a consequence of this transition to a highly selective model. It will be shown how these reforms deeply influenced the daily lives of millions of Chinese families and set the agenda for all other educational reforms. *Chapter 8* takes up the relationship between secondary education and the world of work. The different types of secondary vocational schools and the problems confronting them are presented, as well as the reduced role of labour education in general

---

2. The bibliographic data for the works of these and other authors can be found in the list of books and articles at the end of this book.

schools. The relevance for China of the vocationalization strategy is also discussed. This chapter is partly based on observations made during two stays in Harbin City, Heilongjiang Province.

Chapters 9 and 10 cover the problematic effects of the reforms in two fields to which the Chinese have traditionally paid close attention: Moral education and the educational opportunities of children from different social classes. *Chapter 9* describes the role and content of moral and political education in secondary school and the contradiction between this education and the social realities facing the students. The manifestations of this contradiction during the student demonstrations in the spring and summer of 1989 are also taken up. *Chapter 10* discusses the educational opportunities of children from different social classes and of the two sexes in post-Mao secondary schools. This analysis is mainly based on a questionnaire survey I conducted in six schools of Yantai District, Shandong Province in 1984. It will be shown that the future Chinese elite is mainly recruited from among the children of intellectuals and cadres, but that possibilities for upward social mobility through the school system still exist for the children of workers and peasants. This chapter will also serve as a case study of the implementation of the reforms in one locality in China.

The Social Functions of Secondary Education

Secondary education plays a versatile and important role in China. Secondary schools prepare students for participation in production and society and select them for different careers. In this way, they strongly affect the social distribution process. The Chinese discussion of the reforms has focused almost exclusively on the qualifying function of secondary education. However, any critical discussion of post-Mao secondary education wanting to go behind the officially sponsored myths must take other facets of its social role into account as well. In the following, the key functions of education to be discussed in the present study will be presented.

The qualifying function

The manifest function of Chinese secondary education is to qualify succeeding generations for future participation in society in general and in production in particular. To achieve this aim students must be instilled with ideological and technical qualifications; they must, to use a Chinese phrase, be "red" as well as "experts". *Technical qualifications* include *general* and *specific skills*. Examples of general skills are literacy and basic knowledge of mathematics, physics and the political institutions. Such skills are necessary for all Chinese citizens if they are to take part in the social and political processes at any level. Specific skills, on the other hand, are directly related to the job each individual performs. Technical qualifications are transmitted either through formal education in schools or through informal training carried out by a young person's parents and/or by local craftsmen or others. Technical qualifications, and specific skills in particular, have been constantly stressed as being vital in the Chinese educational debate since 1977. The entire process of streaming and vocationalizing secondary schools, for instance, has been built on the argument that middle school graduates of the Cultural Revolution decade left school without sufficient technical qualifications (cf. Chapter 8).

Besides learning to master certain skills, students are also instilled with *ideological qualifications,* a set of moral and political norms and values preparing them for citizenry in Chinese society.

Part of these ideological qualifications are directly transmitted through formal moral and political education, which takes up a considerable amount of the curriculum in Chinese middle schools, particularly if one includes the subjects of Chinese and History, where the content has a strong moral-political flavour.

This kind of formal ideological education is, however, often of secondary importance compared to what has been called the "hidden curriculum" of the school, i.e. norms and values which are inherent in the educational system, in teaching methods etc..., but which are not specified in official curriculum guidelines and which often work behind the back of teachers and educational planners. Conflicts between the content of formal moral education on one hand and the hidden curriculum on the other are often a source for ideological turmoil inside the minds of the students. For instance, in a competitive school system like that of post-Mao China, students learn to compete with each other even though the virtues of cooperation and mutual help are praised by teachers and textbooks. Likewise, students look down upon manual professions because experience tells them that only those with the lowest examination scores, those who are regarded as failures by the teachers, end up as workers. The textbooks may well tell them that workers are the "masters of the country", but the contradicting message of the hidden curriculum is even stronger.

The selective function

In addition to providing students with technical and ideological qualifications, middle schools also select students for different career paths. All societies with a social division of labour must find ways to distribute jobs with different skill requirements and social prestige, and the criteria used in this selection process are often the object of fierce political and ideological struggle. In China, where a person's level of formal education is, and has traditionally been, a most important determinant for his or her career opportunities, this selective function is primarily carried out by the educational system. Of course it is possible for some to get a better job through family connections or even corruption, but such channels are only open to a minority. Access to education, therefore, plays a crucial role in the selection of young people for different jobs.

Selection takes place at all levels of education, but most important are the screenings carried out between junior and senior secondary school and between senior secondary school and university. In the first of these selections, it is decided who will continue in academic track schools, who will go to the vocational schools leading to jobs as skilled workers and technicians, and who will leave the educational system and find less valued, manual jobs. In the second selection, the few students who will receive a post-secondary education are chosen. These selections (which are the subject of Chapter 7) have even greater social importance in China than in the West, due to the narrowness of alternative routes for upward social mobility in China.

One very important role of the school system's selective function is to provide justification for the social division of labour and the privileges enjoyed by those at the top of the job hierarchy. Those who are placed in subordinate jobs must be made to feel that they have had their chance and that their fate has been justly determined. Therefore, it is essential for the leadership to design a selection system which is legitimate in the eyes of the ordinary citizens.

The social distributive function
Because of its intrinsic and symbolic value, education is also a parameter for welfare. A Chinese family measures its living standard not only by its income level, housing conditions, etc..., but also by the education offered to its children. Educational policies therefore have a direct impact on social distribution and can be used to generate changes in the balance between social classes. The most evident example of this is perhaps the discussion on enrolment criteria for secondary and tertiary education. Up to 1977, education was used in the PRC as an instrument of social redistribution. Children of workers and peasants were given certain privileges in admission to secondary schools and universities, while children from middle and former upper class families were discriminated against (cf. Chapter 7). After 1977, this policy was revoked. During the reform decade the emphasis was on establishing identical, primarily academic, criteria for all regardless of social origin, rather than on securing a proportionate enrolment of

children from different social classes. This revision of admission policies was warmly welcomed by the urban elites, and it is they who have probably benefitted the most from it (cf. Chapter 10).

These three key social functions of secondary education imply that educational policies are closely interdependent with not only the technical aspects of production, but also the organization of production, the relationship between the leaders and the led and social and political questions like social mobility, privileges, and political participation.

These questions have been key areas of political and social struggle in China ever since the victory of the revolution in 1949. Education has therefore been the ground of many serious political conflicts during this period and the victors of these political battles have successively tried different educational models. Chapter 2 is a review of China's experiences with these models.

2. The Historical Development of Secondary Education in China

The aim of this chapter is to trace some of the present problems concerning the social functions of secondary education back to their historical roots and briefly discuss the experiences lying behind present policies. Therefore only the main "historical lessons" to be drawn from each period will be mentioned leaving out the numerous contradictory trends often existing at the same time.[1]

Chinese Education Before 1949

The imperial educational system was not split up into separate parts with distinct social functions. The entire hierarchy of schools and examinations worked as one system, and no part of it had the double function characteristic of modern secondary education of preparing some students for higher education while qualifying others for specific jobs. Each step of the structure prepared students for the next step, and the large majority of students did not make it to the top, and were left with only the general, very useful, tool of literacy, but no specific skills preparing them for any particular job, except, perhaps, for teaching at the lower levels of that same structure. Other types of education of a more vocational orientation did exist, but they were not a recognized part of the official education system.[2]

Many traditional Chinese attitudes to teaching have survived and continue to influence secondary education. Traditionally, teaching has been seen primarily as a way of leading students towards moral superiority, or, in other words, of transmitting ideological qualifications. China's famous "first teacher", Confucius, had little regard for the teaching of practical skills, but was primarily concerned with the perfection of the traditional virtues.[3]

The content of the imperial civil service exams (to which we shall return in more detail in Chapter 7) reflected the same attitude. Students were examined

---

1. Several works describe the development of Chinese education since 1949 in more detail, see i.a. *Löfstedt 1980*, *Price 1979* and *Unger 1982*.

2. These alternative schools are described in *Rawski 1979*.

3. When asked to offer instruction on agriculture for example, Confucius, full of contempt, advised his student to look up an old peasant, cf. *Lun Yü (The Analects)*, XIII, 4.

in the Confucian classics rather than in any practical skills useful in the daily work of an official. The civil service examination system guaranteed a close connection between educational career and social position, as exams, at least in principle, were the only way to officialdom. Moral superiority, a high level of education and a high social rank thus became inseperable concepts in traditional China. High social rank, again, was connected with the right to avoid manual labour, as expressed in the famous saying by Mencius that "Those who labor with their brains govern others; those who work with their brawn are governed by others. Those governed by others feed them. Those who govern others are fed by them".[4]

Transmitting mainly moral values, the teacher was also to be a moral example to his students, and his person thus became the natural center of the teaching situation. He conveyed moral principles recorded in texts which had reached the status of irrefutable dogmas. The most prevalent learning method thus became the word-by-word memorization of these texts. This type of instruction continues to dominate Chinese classrooms.[5]

High social prestige, emphasis on moral instruction, teacher-centered education methods and rote learning are all key characteristics of traditional Chinese education still relevant for a discussion of the distinct features of Chinese education today.

The concept of secondary or middle level education (*zhongdeng jiaoyu*) did not exist in traditional Chinese education but was imported from the West. It was the Western intrusion in China which led to the abolition of the imperial civil service examination system in 1905 and the creation of a modern school system influenced in particular by Japan and USA. In 1922 a structure of six years primary, three years junior and three years senior secondary education was introduced in accordance with the American model.[6]

The Middle School Law (*zhongxue fa*) of 1922 stated that the aim of middle schools was to train students for "all different kinds of occupations" as well as for higher education,[7] and early examples of vocational education could be found

---

4. See *Meng Zi (Mencius)*, IIIa, 4. Translation from *Fung 1952*, p. 114.

5. For an interesting discussion on the role of memorization in Chinese schools after 1949, see *Unger 1982*, pp. 66-82.

6. *Wang 1966*, p. 363.

7. *Jiaoyu Da Cishu*, p. 76.

in Shanghai and other places.[8] As Y.C. Wang points out, however, the large majority of secondary schools were in reality "mere appendages to the colleges and had hardly any importance of their own".[9] Middle school graduates mainly continued into further education or became primary school teachers. Only a smaller proportion went on to other occupations,[10] and these students had in general not been specifically trained for the posts they filled. With few exceptions secondary education before 1949 was geared towards higher education, it was city based and socially highly exclusive, and qualifications for specific vocations had to be acquired outside the secondary school system.

A fundamentally different attitude to education was found in the Communist ruled "base areas". Controlling rather remote and underdeveloped areas of China, the CCP had no use for an educational structure that, at best, trained people either for higher education or for jobs in parts of the public sector in the larger cities. The main emphasis in base area education was on literacy training and primary and adult education. Middle schools were also established, but their main function was to train adults as cadres for the base area administration rather than to train adolescents.[11]

In 1944 new guidelines for base area middle schools were published.[12] The curriculum was to contain subjects locally needed for the training of qualified manpower and the content of each subject was viewed in the light of local production needs. The experiences gained during this period have exerted great influence on later Chinese policies towards secondary education, especially during the Great Leap Forward and the Cultural Revolution. It should be kept in mind, however, that base area schools did not have to select and train people for advanced sectors of the economy or for tertiary education. In spite of their usefulness for raising the general level of education in poor and backward areas and for cadre training they were not a complete answer to the demands put to secondary education in a modern society.

One problem left unsolved by the traditional school system was, however, tackled by the CCP. This was the question of greater social equality in recruitment, which had already been stressed by Mao in his 1927 "*Report on an Investi-*

---

8. For a discussion of some of these early vocational schools see *Risler 1989*, pp. 175-232, and *JYYJ* no. 8, 1985, pp. 23-26.

9. *Wang 1966*, p. 377.

10. *Wang 1966*, p. 376, quoting Shu Xincheng: *Jiaoyu Conggao Di Yi Ji*, Shanghai 1925.

11. Base area education is described in *Selden 1971*, particularly pp. 267-274, and *Wang 1975*.

12. The main points of the guidelines are translated in *Seybolt 1973*, pp. 372-375.

gation of the Peasant Movement in Hunan". Here he complained that "...In China, education has always been the exclusive preserve of the landlords, and the peasants have had no access to it".[13] He realized, however, that "education for all" was a meaningless slogan unless the content of education was changed to fit the needs and preconditions of peasant children. That social redistribution through the educational system was not only a question of bureaucratic rules and admission criteria was thus well known to the CCP leadership long before the victory of the revolution. In Yan'an and other base areas great efforts were made to recruit peasant children into the school system, while at the same time transforming this system to suit their needs, particularly by adapting the curriculum to rural conditions.

From the Revolution to the Great Leap Forward
During the first years after the victory of the revolution in 1949 the Communist government did little to reform the national structure of secondary education in accordance with the base area principles. The system of three years' junior followed by three years' senior secondary school remained untouched, and the curriculum underwent only moderate changes.

Throughout the 1950s the Soviet Union strongly influenced Chinese education but more so at the tertiary than at the secondary level. The tradition for narrow specialization in polytechnical middle schools, however, was a feature taken over from the Soviet model.

A considerable expansion of secondary education took place during this period. According to Chinese statistics middle school enrolment increased from around 1.5 mill. in the pre-revolution peak year to around 6.3 mill. in 1957.[14] At the same time an increasing number of students attended either Workers' and Peasants' Short Course Middle Schools, Vocational Middle Schools or various kinds of spare time schools.[15] These non-formal types of schooling owed more to the base area model than the formal school system did, and often trained people for specific jobs.

The expansion of enrolment made possible a considerable increase in the number of working class students, particularly at primary and secondary level,

---

13. *Mao 1967*, vol. I, p. 53.

14. *Ten Great Years*, p. 192.

15. The decision to implement these kinds of schools is translated in *Hu and Seifman 1976*, pp. 31-33.

and this was seen as an important part of the revolutionary transformation. Already in his annual report for 1950, Minister of Education Ma Xunlun stated:

> Whether in urban or rural districts, the numbers of offspring of workers and peasants' students have increased greatly both in middle and in elementary schools. In the old areas (i.e. the base areas, S.T.) the offsprings of workers and peasants make up some 80 percent of the total number of middle school and elementary school students.[16]

In 1952, a scholarship system was introduced to further accelerate this development.

During the 1950s the proportion of students of worker and peasant origin in general middle schools rose from 51.3% in 1951 to 69.1% in 1957, and the proportion of girls went up from 20% before liberation to 30.8% in 1957. At technical middle schools the worker and peasant children made up 66.6% in 1957 against 56.6% in 1951.[17] Secondary school still had a very exclusive character though. Löfstedt estimates that only around 3.5% of the age cohort were enrolled in general middle school in 1954,[18] and following this estimate no more that 6% of the age group can have been enrolled in 1957. Moreover, schools were still concentrated in towns and cities to a degree that made L.A. Orleans state that "Until 1958, for all practical purposes, there were no middle schools (i.e. secondary schools) in the Chinese countryside".[19] The peasant children who gained access to secondary education normally had to go at least as far as to the nearest county town to receive their education.

There was an obvious demand for all kinds of qualified manpower during this period, and opportunities for higher education or employment were excellent for middle school graduates. Up to 1957 the number of university entrants was, in general, higher than the number of senior middle school graduates. Not until 1957, when tertiary enrolment went down while more students than ever before graduated from senior middle school, did the problem of lack of space in higher education appear. Even in 1962, however, where the pressure on tertiary education was stronger than in any other year before the Cultural Revolution, one in four general senior middle school graduates could enter university. After the re-

16. Ma's speech is translated in *Hu and Seifman* 1976, pp. 23-29. Quotation from p. 23.

17. *Ten Great Years*, pp. 200-201.

18. *Löfstedt 1980*, p. 81.

19. Quoted in *Price 1979*, p. 128.

opening of the universities in 1971, in contrast, not even one in twenty graduates was admitted (cf. Table 2.1).

Already in the early years of the PRC ideological education was mentioned as part of the curriculum at all levels of schooling, but at the same time the Chinese leaders had a very pragmatic attitude towards secondary education, seeing it mainly as a tool of economic development. This is clearly reflected in a report from the National Secondary Education Conference held in 1954, which stated:

> The future problem for the existing schools is not one of remolding but one of progress and development. Under the illumination of the general line, these schools should continue to serve the socialist construction enterprise and keep the nation supplied with a regular flow of construction personnel. At the same time, on the foundation of production development, they should work for the continued and incessant elevation of the cultural level of the people and their socialist awakening...
>
> In order to cope with the demand for the socialist industrialization of the nation, greater importance should in principle be attached to the development of senior middle schools than that of junior middle schools and of those in the big cities and industrial and mining districts than those in ordinary districts.[20]

In this document, the principal function of secondary education is clearly seen as the transfer of technical qualifications, while ideological education receives less attention. The idea of using education as an instrument of social redistribution, for example to level out disparities between town and countryside or between manual and mental labour, is absent.

The Great Leap Forward

During the Great Leap Forward from 1958 to 1959 three trends appeared that deeply influenced the social functions of Chinese secondary education.

First of all the expansion of enrolment was strongly accelerated, the number of students in general middle schools going up from 6.3 mill. in 1957 to 9.2 mill. in 1959.[21] The expansion took place in the general spirit of exaggerated optimism during the Leap, but it confronted a very real problem: The ambitious

---

20. Translated in *Hu and Seifman 1976*, pp. 66-69. Quotation from p. 67.

21. *Zhongguo Jiaoyu Nianjian 1949-1981*, p. 1001.

political and economic aims of the Leap would be impossible to reach without raising the general level of technical and ideological qualifications.

Secondly, a large number of "half-work - half-study" schools were established, especially in the countryside. This was a precondition for the expansion in enrolment, an expansion which could not have taken place had the cost of schooling not been reduced. These part-time schools needed much fewer resources and their curriculum could be easily adapted to local needs, but the academic standard was, of course, lower than in the full-time schools, and they did in this way represent a non-academic track inside the secondary school system. At the other end of the quality scale, "key point" or elite schools existed, where a concentration of resources was to, in Zhou Enlai's words, lead to training of "specialized personnel of higher quality for the state...".[22] Roughly speaking the part-time and spare-time schools played the same role as the base area middle schools had done in training locally needed qualified personnel, while the full-time schools continued to fill the traditional role of middle schools in China, namely that of preparing students for higher education and white collar jobs.

The division of middle schools into tracks with different social functions reflected the actual division of labour within the society. An uncritical expansion of the academically oriented, city-based middle school system into the rural areas would have been both impossible to implement due to insufficient supply of teachers and funds and without purpose, since it could not provide peasant children with the skills needed in agricultural production. This point seems to have been supported by both Liu Shaoqi and Mao Zedong, and the Great Leap reforms were considered progressive also in later Cultural Revolution evaluations in spite of this indirect streaming.[23] The division between full-time and part-time schools did, however, raise new questions on the ideological and political front. It made the selective function of secondary school very obvious. The kind of middle school attended decided future career opportunities. In a period of expansion, where underprivileged groups and areas went from no access to secondary education to *some* access to *some* kind of secondary schooling the prospect of inequity did not cause social tension. Later, however, when educational opportunities were reduced, such tension arose.

---

22. *Chou 1959*, p. 38.

23. See *"Chronology of the Two-Road Struggle on the Educational Front in the Past Seventeen Years"* translated in *Seybolt 1973*, pp. 5-60, particularly pp. 29-39 for the Great Leap years. Here Liu Shaoqi is accused of "regarding half-study and half-work as his own innovation" (p. 33), which indicates that he as well as Mao promoted this kind of schools.

Finally, physical labour was introduced as an important part of the curriculum. Students' participation in productive labour was seen not only as an economic and pedagogical necessity but also as a way to bridge the gap between the different tracks of the educational system. This is expressed clearly in Chinese statements from this period:

> The coordination of education with labour is a general principle. Under the guidance of this general principle we should coordinate theory with practice and physical labour with brain exertion in the simultaneous pursuit of studies and labor, so that the intellectual elements can be welded with the mass of workmen and peasants.[24]

Negative consequences of the social division of labour and the subsequent tracking of the students were thus to be reduced by student participation in physical labour. The question of whether physical labour in middle schools should be restricted to spare-time and vocational schools, where it was necessary for economic as well as for pedagogical reasons, or should be extended to academic track full-time schools as well, has been a much debated issue in China ever since.

During the Leap, children from peasants' and workers' families benefited from the rapid expansion of the educational sector. If statistics from that time can be trusted, their share of the places went up to 75.2% in general middle schools and 77% in polytechnical middle schools.[25] No data exist, however, on the distribution of children of different social origin in different categories and qualities of schools.

The Early 1960s

During the first half of the 1960s, the multi-track system was developed and formalized. The different tracks now openly aimed at preparing students for different jobs. Agricultural middle schools and work-study schools in the villages trained manpower for the agricultural sector, vocational and specialized middle schools trained skilled workers and middle level technicians for the industrial and

---

24. Dong Zunzai: "Two Major Reform Measures on General Education", *RMJY* no. 4, 1958. Translated in *Hu and Seifman 1976*, pp. 93-96. Quotation from p. 95.

25. *Ten Great Years*, p. 200.

service sectors, while students from urban full-time general middle schools competed for access to tertiary education.[26]

This "two-kinds-of-education-system" (*liang zhong jiaoyu zhidu*) associated with Liu Shaoqi probably reflected the demand for qualified manpower on one hand and the limited resources on the other, and was, in this way, an economically rational response to the problems confronting secondary education. But it did not conform with the egalitarian visions of Mao and other radicals, and its political and ideological effects were, from their point of view, far from ideal.

First of all, the question of securing equal access to education for the offspring of workers and peasants was not solved. Class origin was taken into consideration when students were enrolled in middle school,[27] but while this to some degree screened out children of former capitalists and landlords, it did little to help students from proletarian families gain access to schools. It was mainly children of cadre and intelligentsia middle class origin who benefited from the combination of academic and political criteria used in the selection of students for the best "key" middle schools. Jonathan Unger concludes: "Different "classes" of youths, in short, were concentrated at secondary schools of different qualities".[28] This again influenced social recruitment to higher education and created a basis for later Cultural Revolution critique of the system as "bourgeois".

The system failed to bridge the gap between urban and rural areas as well. As late as 1965, only 33.7% of junior and 9% of senior middle school students attended village schools,[29] in spite of the fact that more than 80% of the population were living in the villages. The village schools, moreover, were primarily of the "half-work - half-study" type.

Secondly, the full-time schools trained students whose qualifications, at least from the point of view of Mao and his supporters, were far from perfect. The belief in "quality" led to a one-sided emphasis on fundamental theoretical knowledge, book learning and individual achievement.[30] The Maoist critique of

---

26. The educational system of the early sixties is described in *Löfstedt 1980*, *Price 1979*, *Shirk 1982* and *Unger 1982*.

27. For the changes in the relative importance of political, academic and class criteria in the sixties see *Unger 1982*, pp. 12-16 and *Shirk 1982*, pp. 41-56.

28. *Unger 1982*, p. 26.

29. *Achievement of Education*, p. 197. For the distribution of schools on rural and urban areas from 1962 to 1987 see Table 6.3.

30. For an elaboration of these points see *Shirk 1973*.

this point is well known: The students became book-worms who were unable to put their knowledge into practice.

Thirdly, the hidden curriculum of middle schools in this period tended to make students' ideology differ considerably from the official lines. As political activism was one way to further one's career the problem of "phoney activism" and hypocrisy arose. Academic competition, on the other hand, was in contradiction to official propaganda regarding comradeship and serving the people. The educational system of the early sixties was, in short, "unsuccessful in using the schools to transform social relations to fit the Maoist vision".[31] Ideological education could not cover up the fact that one important objective function of the schools was to select some students for higher education and, implicitly, for elite status.

These flaws of the educational system of the early 1960s were probably only seen as such by the radical wing of the CCP, which would shortly thereafter initiate the Cultural Revolution. Others, among them Deng Xiaoping and other moderate leaders, saw it as a well-functioning and stable system preparing the people needed for socialist construction. The resemblance between this system and the system created by the reforms after Mao's death is striking. This may partly be due to lack of alternative visions on the side of the reform leaders, but it also shows that they, and many of those who were students and teachers in the early 1960s, recollect this time with affection, in spite of all of its, as Mao saw it, ideological shortcomings.

The Decade of the Cultural Revolution (1966-1976)

The middle school system that was gradually established in the early 1970s after the first tumultuous years of the Cultural Revolution[32] gave its own radical answers to the questions posed by the 1960s. A proletarian school system should actively transform and not just reflect the existing division of labour. Consequently, all students should in principle receive the same kind of education, and the selective function of middle schools should be abolished. The total period of schooling was cut down from twelve to (in most areas) ten years, consisting of five years of primary school, three years of junior secondary and two years of senior secondary school. Long stints of manual labour were included in the curriculum. School administration was transferred to lower levels, often to

---

31. *Shirk 1982*, p. 179.

32. For the sake of simplicity I use the phrase "Cultural Revolution" here to describe the whole period from 1966 to 1976, not just the few years of revolutionary activism.

enterprises or brigades. Almost all vocational schools were converted into general schools, and the "key school" system was abolished. Large numbers of middle school graduates were sent to settle in the villages, some of them for good, and entrance to higher education depended no longer on middle school achievements or examination scores but on recommendations from one's work unit. This transferred the selective function from the educational system, which in Mao's eyes was dominated by bourgeois intellectuals, to the factories and people's communes.

While not only the content and structure but the entire social role of secondary education in this way was changed, middle school enrolment increased at the same time at a unprecedented rate. In 1965, there were only around 18,000 general middle schools in China with 9.3 mill. students. In 1977, the number had risen to more than 200,000 schools with nearly 68 mill. students.[33] This expansion was particularly impressive in rural schools, which in 1977 enrolled 78% of all junior and 66% of all senior middle school students.[34]

Instead of preparing some students for tertiary education and others for manual jobs or other vocations, the middle schools of the early seventies aimed at providing all students with a common set of ideological qualifications (political education took up much time for all students) as well as with technical qualifications which could be adapted to local needs, but which should be identical for future mental and manual workers. In the ideal society envisioned by the Maoists productive labour was to be performed by all, not only in school, but also in later work life. They believed that any selection of students based on academic criteria would cement existing disparities in society. Also important for the Maoist reforms was their vision of a future dominated by small, technologically uncomplicated local enterprises, where the need for manpower trained at a high theoretical level was not very acute, but where practical, applicable skills were in high demand.

The main aims of the reforms, aside from the rather abstract slogan of "revolutionizing students' ideology", were to break the connection between middle school performance and career prospects and to establish a close linkage between book learning and participation in productive labour. In the view of later attacks on Cultural Revolution educational policies it is worth noting that reforms along these lines were actually in accordance with the recommendations of many Western experts in the educational systems of developing countries.

---

33. *Zhongguo Jiaoyu Nianjian 1949-1981*, pp. 1000-1001.

34. *Achievement of Education*, p. 197.

They saw investments in exam-oriented general middle schools as one of the main evils of educational policies in many former European colonies. China had avoided the "diploma disease" and followed a line in educational policy, which in many ways was close to the recommendations put forward by UNESCO.[35]

The implications of these policies for the social distribution are difficult to estimate, as there are no systematic statistics on the class background of either middle school or university students for this period, but as enrolment went up and middle school students were enrolled according to the district in which they lived and not according to academic aptitude, a high degree of equality was most likely reached at this level of schooling. This was not necessarily the case in higher education, where there were now fewer opportunities than in the sixties. Gordon White has looked at the scattered pieces of information on this topic and reached the conclusion that children of urban workers kept or perhaps marginally enlarged their share of the places at university. Middle class children lost some ground, and this tendency was even stronger among children of the old exploiting classes. For the peasants there was no real progress, as a large part of the new "peasant-students" were in reality urban children who had spent some years in a village. The offspring of cadres seem to have been the only group who really benefitted from the new system.[36] This conclusion is supported by Chinese intellectuals, who frequently accuse cadres, today as well as during the Cultural Revolution, of slipping their own children into university "through the back door", if they have the slightest opportunity to do so. This highlights a basic dilemma of Chinese admissions policy which has gained new relevance in the 1980s: if other than rigid, objective criteria are used, the privileged strata of Chinese society will score the profit by mobilizing their connection network (*guanxi wang*).

Critique of Cultural Revolution Secondary Education
In October 1976, the Cultural Revolution leadership, symbolized by the "Gang of Four", was overthrown, and new political leaders came into power whose views on education differed widely from Cultural Revolution principles. The educational field was regarded as one of the main strongholds of the "Gang", and after their fall deep-going reforms were implemented.

---

35. Ronald P. Dore used the phrase "the diploma disease" to describe the situation in most developing countries, but found, like many others, that China had taken a more promising course. See *Dore 1976*.

36. *White 1981*.

To understand the motives behind the middle school reforms of the late 1970s, it is necessary to look at the charges made against Cultural Revolution secondary education by the new leaders. These charges were only gradually developed, as political conflicts between different groups inside the new leadership were solved and the reform wing of the CCP gained control over political decision-making.[37] Today, the main points of critique can be summarized as follows:

1. The extremely rapid expansion of secondary education and particularly of senior middle school led to a disastrous decline in the quality of education, because economic as well as human resources were strained beyond capacity.

2. As a result of the lack of qualified teachers, and because all students, even the unqualified, were accepted in senior middle school, the academic level of the students fell drastically.

3. By turning vocational and agricultural schools into general schools, Cultural Revolution reforms created a work force without specific job-related skills. What the country really needed were young people who had acquired concrete job qualifications when they left middle school, so that the training period at the work place could be minimized.

4. Because of the anarchy present in many schools and because middle school achievement had no influence on later career prospects, the morale of the students was low, and many of them did not study at all.

The first of these points has been documented by statistics showing that while the number of middle school students at the end of the Cultural Revolution was 5.57 times higher than in 1965, expenditures only rose 1.58 times during the same period, so that the annual expenditure per student fell from 88.89 yuan in 1965 to 36.42 yuan in 1976. Funds for basic construction works in education were also inadequate and made up a declining proportion of total expenditures on basic construction.[38] This led to problems of inadequate housing and equipment at most schools. Even in Beijing, where conditions were better than in most other cities and far better than in the countryside, the average school building area per

---

37. I use the term "reform wing" here to describe the alliance of pro-reform factions headed by Deng Xiaoping which gained power at the 3rd Plenum of the 11th Party Congress in December 1978.

38. *Wu and Zhang 1981.*

student in primary and secondary school was as low as 3.2 square meters in 1979, 0.7 square meters less than in 1949.[39]

Teachers' training also lagged behind the expansion in enrolment. Many former primary school teachers were transferred to middle schools, and senior and even junior middle school graduates were often appointed teachers at junior middle schools without having received any pedagogical training. A breakdown by level of education of the middle school teaching force (cf. Table 2.2) clearly demonstrates its low level of formal education in 1978 as well as the considerable upgrading taking place during the reform decade. Even in Beijing, only half of the middle school teachers were considered qualified for their job in 1980.[40] There is thus ample evidence that the allocation of resources to secondary education did not keep pace with the expansion in enrolment.

As to the second point, the qualifications of Cultural Revolution middle school graduates have often been thrown into doubt by the Chinese press during the reform period. Their low academic level has been documented by their poor performance in academic tests. We have been told, for example, that in the first years after the fall of the "Gang of Four", only around 30% of all junior middle school graduates were up to the required standards as compared to 50-60% in the late 1980s.[41]

Such data must, however, be looked upon with great caution. The tests used naturally follow the criteria of the present examination system with its heavy emphasis on abstract knowledge and memorization. Cultural Revolution ideas on education stressed, at least in theory, totally different values such as political consciousness and the ability to apply acquired skills, and these qualifications are not tested today.

There is, however, little doubt that the reduction of primary school from six to five years and of senior middle school from three to two years, the time-consuming political indoctrination, and the long stints of manual labour of a more or less ritualistic nature all contributed to a decrease in academic standards.

The third charge, lack of vocational preparation, is correct in the sense that vocational training inside the formal education system was strongly reduced during the Cultural Revolution decade. On the other hand the practical aspects of the general curriculum were strengthened. As we shall see later, international experiences with vocational vs. general education at the secondary level are far

---

39. *JYYJ* no. 6, 1981, pp. 45-48.

40. Ibid.

41. *Zhongguo Baike Nianjian 1988*, p. 480.

from uniform (cf. Chapter 8), and it is still an open question whether the present vocationalization strategy will be successful. If we look at rural schools in particular, the agricultural middle schools established in the early 1980s build on the same basic principle as the Cultural Revolution general schools, i.e. a combination of academic subjects and agricultural theory and practice (cf. Chapter 8). Blankly stating that Cultural Revolution schools did not prepare students for their later jobs is thus an oversimplification.

The fourth point, low morale of the students, was probably a very real problem. Jonathan Unger's interviews with emigrants and refugees document this tendency. Unger started from the hypothesis that "...if an educational system could be divorced from the competition for careers...students would be better able to learn for intrinsic reasons", but he had to conclude that students' interest in learning declined in Canton in the early seventies, and that the conditions in many schools were quite chaotic, a picture closely resembling the one propagated in the Chinese press after the fall of the 'Gang of Four'.[42]

Thus, the strong charges against Cultural Revolution secondary education voiced by the reform wing were partly justified but also strongly politically motivated. Ideas were put forth and experiments carried out during that period which addressed some very real problems of Chinese educational tradition and of the system of the early 1960s: The social exclusiveness of schooling, the separation of theory from practice, and the rigidity of teaching methods. The system was no doubt overstrained, and many new ideas degenerated into pure formalism because of the lack of human and material resources to implement them properly and due to the extreme degree of political control. But it did prove quite successful in expanding educational opportunities, particularly in rural areas and among women (cf. Tables 6.1, 6.3 and 6.4). An emotionally detached evaluation of secondary education during the Cultural Revolution decade and of the general and specific skills acquired by the young generation during that period would be useful to bring out the merits and drawbacks of such a radical approach.

The "Historical Lessons"
Due to the pendular movements of educational policies during the period from 1949 to 1976, China had extensive experiences with different models upon which the post-Mao leadership could build their own reform program. Put in a schematic way, the academic and selective model had proved unable to level out

---

42. *Unger 1982*, p. 171.

disparities between social classes and between urban and rural areas. This model was also connected, historically if not logically, with a traditional teaching style stressing memorization. The curriculum had a strong theoretical bias, and, at least in general schools, few attempts were made to develop students' practical skills. Finally, the model led to contradictions between egalitarian rhetoric and competitive practice.

When, on the other hand, education was seen mainly as an agent of social change, as was the case during the Cultural Revolution, it was expanded and made available to a much larger part of the population. In this way economic and human resources were strained beyond capacity, however, and the quality of education dropped. Though middle school lost its selective function, a division of labour still existed in society and the absence of objective selection criteria led to nepotism and bias towards children of the political elite. This reduced students' motivation because better academic results did not bring them better jobs. Moreover, the tense, often hysterical political climate of this period and the many underqualified teachers, whom it was necessary to employ because of the rapid expansion, often turned teaching into pure political liturgy.

Both models had their own drawbacks, and they both created tension in Chinese society. When, however, the post-Mao leaders from 1977 onwards carried out their own reforms of secondary education, they decided to follow the model of the early 1960s very closely, even sharpening some particularly controversial points. This choice, which led secondary education into all the same pitfalls as in the early 1960s, only on an even larger scale, was heavily influenced by the general political and ideological climate in China after the fall of the "Gang of Four", and that is the subject of the next chapter.

3. The Political and Ideological Framework for Educational Reforms

When the "Gang of Four" were arrested in October 1976, a new epoch in the history of the People's Republic began. Hua Guofeng, Mao's immediate successor as chairman of the CCP, had risen to prominence during the Cultural Revolution and felt bonded to at least some of its policies. At the Third Plenum of the Eleventh Party Congress in December 1978, however, the reform wing of the Party, headed by Deng Xiaoping, gained the upper hand, and the ideology of the Party as well as its policies in almost every field subsequently underwent rapid change.

The field of education has been no exception. Educational reforms have been in full harmony with the basic orientation of the whole reform process and the educational sector has even been a display window, where some of the reform principles have first been presented. Though both economic and political reforms have gone through many ups and downs during the ten years since 1978,[1] some basic ideological and political trends can be identified in the statements made by the leaders as well as in the much more indefinable "public opinion". I shall sum up the most important trends below in five points: the total negation of the Cultural Revolution and the return to power of the pre-1966 elite; the shift of the focus of the Party's work from class struggle to economic modernization and the call for national unity across class boundaries; the new emphasis on material incentives and competition as motivating factors and on objective rather than subjective criteria; the changed role of the Party and its experiments with introducing new ways of popular participation in political life without giving up its ultimate monopoly of power, and, finally, the opening up of the country for contacts with the industrialized world. These five points do not cover the whole spectrum of ideological and political change in China since 1978, but they have,

---

1. A great number of books and articles on reforms in China after Mao have been published in the past few years. *Harding 1987* is a competent work which provides an overview of the process. For the ideological debates see in particular *Schram 1984* and *Schram 1987*. *Brugger 1986* contains an interesting comparison of the ideology of the Cultural Revolution leftists with that of the radical reformers.

it seems to me, been the most essential for the formulation and implementation of the reforms in secondary education.

Return of the Old Elite

Cadres and intellectuals, who had been persecuted and dismissed during the Cultural Revolution, have been rehabilitated in great numbers since 1977, and have formed an important part of the power base of the reform wing from the onset of the reform process. Deng Xiaoping himself reappeared as vice-chairman of the CCP in 1977, and in the spring of 1980 the highest ranking target of the Cultural Revolution, China's president up to 1967, Liu Shaoqi, was posthumously rehabilitated. When Hua Guofeng was removed from his post as Party chairman in 1981, it marked the final victory over the Mao loyalists by the people associated with the pre-1966 period. The political credo of the victors was clearly stated: The Cultural Revolution had been a disaster for China's development in all fields, while pre-1966 policies had been "basically" correct and the period before the Anti-Rightist Campaign of 1957 was pictured as a paradise lost.[2]

On the educational front this development could be observed even earlier. One of the first signs of change was a vehement attack on the so-called "two estimates". During the Cultural Revolution, the pre-1966 educational line had been described as bourgeois and "black", and the majority of the intellectuals were seen as enemies of the people. In 1977, both of these estimates were reversed: Chinese educational policies had been fundamentally correct even in the most "Liuist" period in the early sixties, and the large majority of Chinese intellectuals had been loyal to the Party and to socialism. This viewpoint led to the rehabilitation of most of the educational cadres and teachers criticized during the Cultural Revolution and the Anti-Rightist Campaign and to a positive re-evaluation of the educational policies of Liu Shaoqi.

Concurrently, "new-born things" and model units of the Cultural Revolution came under attack, as did the heroes of that period. Zhang Tiesheng, for example, who had become famous by handing in a blank examination paper as a demonstration against the examination system, was now called "an ignorant, reactionary clown" by Deng Xiaoping.[3]

The rehabilitation of pre-1966 leaders and their policies and the corresponding total rejection of all phenomena associated with the Cultural Revolution have thus been prominent features of the political and ideological development

---

2. For the official evaluation of CCP history up to 1981 see *Resolution on CPC History*.

3. *Deng 1984*, p. 107.

since 1977. This does not mean, of course, that the last ten years simply have been a return to the pre-Cultural Revolution state of affairs. Many policies are genuinely new, but it has been of major importance to the rehabilitated leaders and cadres that the pre-1966 period is seen as a prosperous and harmonious time, while the Cultural Revolution, during which the same cadres experienced political and personal humiliation, is now remembered as an unjustifiable and disastrous event.

In the educational field, the pressure on the post-1977 leadership to return to the legacy of the period before the "ten years of turmoil" and to deny that any trace of sense was present in the ideas and experiments of the Cultural Revolution was even stronger than in other spheres because the teachers, or at least a considerable part of them, had endured sufferings and humiliations similar to, or even worse than, those suffered by the cadres. To secure their cooperation it was necessary to convince them that the new leadership was fully on their side and intended to correct all the wrongs perpetrated against them.

The campaign style of Chinese politics thus blocked a careful and objective assessment of both the positive and negative aspects of the educational experiments that took place during the Cultural Revolution. The Cultural Revolution had had such a tremendous impact on its many victims that, once back in power, they were determined to wipe out all traces of the preceding decade. In reconstructing the educational system it was only natural that they should look to the only model with which they were personally familiar: that of the pre-1966 period.

From Class Struggle to Economic Construction

Another important element of the post-1977 ideological changes is the revised analysis of the principal contradiction in Chinese society and of its class structure. Mao and the Cultural Revolution leaders saw China as a class society, where the struggle between the proletariat and a new bourgeoisie determined the future of the revolution. This new bourgeoisie had, though Mao himself was ambiguous on this point, its social roots inside the Party, i.e. among privileged and corrupt cadres who had lost their proletarian orientation.[4] The intellectuals were another important recruitment base for the bourgeois forces. This was used to justify a relentless political and ideological suppression of the intellectuals, whose "world outlook" was to be transformed by the workers and peasants. It also led to the implementation of a number of radical policies aiming at leveling

---

4. *Christensen and Delman 1981.*

out differences between manual and mental labour, such as the practice of sending middle school graduates to the countryside for several years before allowing them to enter university. Furthermore, it focused political attention on such questions as inequality, students' social background, the political attitude of teachers etc....

As the cadres and intellectuals rehabilitated after 1977 had themselves been pointed out as members of the "bourgeois headquarters", it came as no surprise that they revised this analysis as soon as they were back in power. They saw the principal contradiction after the socialist transformation as "that between the growing material and cultural needs of the people and the backwardness of social production".[5] This meant that the Party should now focus its work on the modernization of the economy. In fact almost all the leading figures in China since the Opium Wars, including Mao Zedong and the Cultural Revolution leftists, have wanted to develop China economically, to make China strong and prosperous. The leftists believed, however, that class struggle had to be carried out in order to safeguard China's socialist orientation, which was, in the final analysis, the only guarantee for continued economic progress. The reform wing, on the other hand, wanted to unite all social strata in a national struggle for economic development. Science and education were seen as crucial elements in the modernization process, and the cooperation of the intellectuals was therefore essential for the success of the new strategy.

To secure their continued cooperation, the intellectuals had to be cleared from all suspicion of being "bourgeois", and be recognized as part of the working class, so that humiliating re-education could not again be inflicted on them. At a national science conference in March, 1978, Deng Xiaoping recognized that class struggle continue to exist all through the socialist period and that intellectuals had to choose side in the struggle, but he then continued:

But generally speaking, the overwhelming majority of them are already intellectuals serving the working class and other working people. It can therefore be said that they are already part of the working class itself. They differ from the manual workers only insofar as they perform different roles

5. *Resolution on CPC History*, p. 76. The "shift of focus" was one of the main contradictions between Hua Guofeng and the reform wing at the Third Plenum, cf. *Schram 1987*, pp. 26-27. For a detailed discussion of the implications of the question of "principal contradiction" see *Sullivan 1985*.

in the social division of labour. Everyone who works, whether with his hands or with his brain, is part of the working people in a socialist country.[6]

It goes without saying that the cadres were also considered members of the working class. This was, however, consistent with Cultural Revolution practices.

The liberation of intellectuals from the discriminations of the preceding decades was, of course, a positive aspect of the reform policies in both political and economic terms. When teachers, for example, were no longer subject to strict political surveillance and even suspicion, they could, at least in principle, feel more free to experiment with new teaching methods and curriculum contents without fearing that any deviance from orthodoxy might lead them into personal disaster. This no doubt made many teachers work harder and more enthusiastically.

But once again, in its swing away from leftist extremes the pendulum effectively blocked the debate not only on education as an instrument of social redistribution but also on the effect of educational reforms on social stratification. As all talk of students' class background and inequality of opportunities became associated with the Cultural Revolution, arguments based on social and political considerations could be brushed aside as being leftist deviations running counter to the principal task of economic construction. This led to the ironic situation that while the sociology of education as an academic discipline was revived after 1978, almost no research was carried out on how differences in students' social background influenced school performance, on how such differences could be overcome, on the effects of educational reforms on peasant children, etc.... It became practically illegitimate to use arguments from the arsenal of the Marxist or critical traditions of the sociology of education in the debate on educational reforms.

Competition and Objective Criteria
The post-1978 economic reforms have given a greater role to market mechanisms and have introduced a number of policies aimed at rewarding the skills, intelligence and diligence of individuals. The new methods of distribution have been seen as manifestations of the principle of "to each according to his work", which was Marx's formula for social distribution at the socialist stage. The inequalities rising from the market economy and the revised distribution mechanisms have

---

6. Deng's speech at the conference is translated in *Deng 1984*, pp. 101-116, quotation from p. 105.

been considered to be an important motivating factor in the modernization process.

In industry, the new principle is evident at the employee level, where bonuses and other work-related payments have constituted an important part of workers' salaries, in contrast to during the Cultural Revolution when they were based mainly on seniority and political attitudes. It is also visible at the enterprise level, where the management, at least in principle, has been made responsible for profits and losses. This should lead to more competition between enterprises and, it is hoped, to more efficiency and a better quality of products. In the countryside the principle of "to each according to his work" has been carried even further, and there is little, except the formal ownership of land, that separates the organization of agriculture in China today from individual farming under a market economy. One of the slogans of this liberalization of the rural economy has been "let some get rich first", where the word "first" expresses the belief that while the new policies will initially lead to greater inequality, those who get rich first will be able to lead others to prosperity later.

The same mechanism is expected to work at the interregional and interprovincial levels where the more advanced coastal areas have been allowed to develop at a faster pace than the poorer inland provinces, in the hope that the advanced areas can pull the whole of China towards prosperity. At the enterprise level "key" plants are expected to fulfill a similar locomotive function.

The employment system, which is of great importance to the educational sector, has also been changed. The system of life-long employment for industrial workers in state-owned enterprises, the so-called "iron rice-bowl", has been challenged and attempts have been made to replace it with a contract system, which should make it easier for enterprises to get rid of unproductive or undisciplined workers. This process has met much opposition and made slow progress. We shall return to this in the discussion of the vocationalization of secondary education, but it deserves mention here as a typical example of the attacks on former strongholds of egalitarianism in the cities, in this case absolute job security.

To make the reforms work, the CCP had to find new objective criteria for evaluating human activities. During the Cultural Revolution all phenomena were analyzed in moral and political terms, at least at the official level: were they good or bad for the revolution? Though most people probably ceased to believe in the official values at an early state of the Cultural Revolution, there were no alternative terms of reference which could be used in the public debate. After 1978, the CCP did not have the political strength to define a new set of values, the general mood being against the acceptance of incontroversible truths defined from above. What could be accepted were objective, or seemingly objective, criteria, principally economic ones. Deng Xiaoping's emphasis on Mao's statement that "practice is the sole criterion of truth" can be seen as a more sophisticated formulation of this standpoint. As economic development was the main aim of the Party, "practice" easily became identified with economic profitability, and "objective economic laws" became the most important yardstick for evaluating all activities. Likewise, educational reforms have often been described as being based on the "objective laws of education", thus trying to move discussions on education from the political to the technical sphere.

That the qualifications of individuals ought to be measured by similar objective criteria rather than by what the Party or individual cadres regarded as desirable behaviour was a parallel demand shared by large sectors of the population, and it deeply influenced the course of educational reforms in the direction of a test and exam oriented system. This tendency has been fittingly described by Susan Shirk as part of a move from virtuocratic to meritocratic values,[7] but objectivization can be seen spreading even into the realm of virtue as reflected by the attempts to use objective criteria in the evaluation of students' political and moral behaviour.[8]

Political Participation and the Role of the Party

As an educational system trains citizens, not just manpower, the nature of China's political system strongly influences the socialization process going on in the schools and vice versa. The question of popular participation in political life, not only at the national level but also in local communities and at the workplaces, is therefore important for the discussion of educational reforms.

In the political field, the reform decade has been characterized by a high degree of liberalization. Intellectual freedom has been much greater than during the Cultural Revolution; heated debates on social, economic and cultural questions have flourished in magazines and newspapers and controversial viewpoints have been widely tolerated. This loosening up of control should, however, not be confused with political pluralism. The Democracy Movement which was active during the liberal period following the Third Plenum in 1978 tested the limits of political freedom. Its eventual suppression demonstrated that Deng Xiaoping still demanded from all participants in the political arena that they remain within the boundaries of the "four cardinal principles" (socialism, the

---

7. *Shirk 1982.*

8. *Bakken 1989* contains a very interesting discussion of this point on pp. 187-200.

40

dictatorship of the proletariat, the leading role of the CCP and Marxism-Leninism-Mao Zedong Thought). This meant, in reality, that the CCP intended to keep firm control over all aspects of China's political and ideological life, and that no independent organization fighting for alternative political aims or for the aims of specific interest groups would be permitted. Since then periods of relative laxness of political control have alternated with campaigns against "spiritual pollution" or "bourgeois liberalization", but the Party has always retained complete political and ideological supremacy. The brutal crushing of the pro-democracy demonstrations in June 1989 is the most recent illustration of this.

People's congresses have been established at several levels and have been used as forums for critique of Party policies and of abuse of power by its individual members, but the few candidates who have tried to base their campaign on an independent political program have quickly found themselves blocked. At the enterprise level, workers' congresses were set up as instruments of workers' control over production after the abolishment of the revolutionary committees, but though they received much publicity particularly around 1981, they seem to have played a very limited role in the enterprise management system of the 1980s.

Political freedom has thus been kept within rather narrow confines, and has been granted to the citizens by the state only to the extent in which it would promote the main objective: economic modernization. The attitude of the Chinese leaders towards democracy is pragmatic and instrumental: if scientists are so effectively suppressed that they dare not forward original ideas and theories, scientific development will stagnate; if certain legal, economic rights are not given to peasants and entrepreneurs they will have no incentive to work harder; if workers are not guaranteed some degree of participation in management they will make trouble. Thus only the minimum amount of democracy necessary for economic development has been granted. The political reforms have consequently been in full accordance with the traditional Chinese attitude towards democracy[9] and did not break with established patterns of authority. If the Party has partially loosened its grip on Chinese society during the last ten years, as seems to be the case, this should not be regarded as an integrated part of the political visions and aspirations of the CCP leadership, but rather as a consequence of both its low prestige and its economic policies. A good example of this is the loss of control over peasants' social life that followed agricultural de-collectivization.

---

9. See *Nathan 1986* for a discussion of this point.

This limited concept of democracy has profound implications for the ideological qualifications transmitted in secondary schools because it puts narrow constraints on the liberalization of political socialization. As the Party claims to know the absolute "truth" in ideological and moral matters, and as it expects its citizens to only take part in the political process to a rather limited extent, it has had no incentive to actively reform teacher-centered teaching methods or to encourage the development of independent thinking, critical sense etc... in the students. Even less so if one considers that not only the political aims but also the whole tradition of Chinese education have worked against such reforms.

Opening to the Western World

China's opening up to the outside world has had a direct impact on the educational system. Thousands of Chinese students have received training abroad during the reform period, Western educational theories have been introduced into China, and international organizations like the World Bank have become directly involved in the development of Chinese education.

However, because China's primary focus has been on economic modernization, the attention of the reformers has been directed towards the industrialized countries rather than towards countries in the Third World whose educational problems in many ways bear more resemblance to China's. The Chinese leaders and probably the majority of the urban population have seen their country as being on the road to industrialization and modernization. It has therefore been natural for them to look to the Western world for educational models. These models have had little to offer to China's rural areas, however, where the level of development is still very low.

Conclusion

The general political and ideological trends of the reform period have put a number of external constraints on educational reforms. These reforms have had to take the legacy of the early 1960s as their frame of reference and firmly reject policies associated with the Cultural Revolution. Moreover, they have had to stress the economic role of education rather than its role as potential agent of social and political change, and to emphasize the technical qualifications of the students and the creation of a more vocationally oriented system. In this process there has been little room for considering the ideological, distributive or political consequences of the reforms. Selection criteria have had to be objectivized and the role of ideology downplayed, while the traditional teacher-centered, authoritarian teaching style has been maintained. Finally, the reforms have been strongly influenced by the experiences of the industrialized Western countries.

As it will be shown in Chapters 5 to 10, the educational reforms worked out under these constraints have not exactly created a state of harmony in secondary education. Quite to the contrary, the educational system has run into extremely serious problems, and they still await solution.

A crucial reason underlying these problems has been the widespread and partly justified feeling in Chinese society that education was becoming the most important ladder for upward social mobility. This has turned much of the attention of students, parents and local educational bureaucracies away from the issue of the applicability of the qualifications transmitted in the middle schools. Instead, the focus has been on how to improve the communication to the students of formal, academic knowledge useful in the key school and university entrance examinations. In Chapter 4, we shall examine more closely the connection between formal education and social status in post-Mao China.

4. Education and Social Status

As this chapter will show, the correlation between educational level and social status in China has become stronger up through the 1980s. This represents a change compared to earlier periods in the People's Republic, where the elite primarily had been composed of cadres with political and military merits but little formal education.

This chapter will examine the importance of formal education for social prestige, political status, job opportunities, income and living conditions in post-Mao China. I shall argue that while education has definitely become more decisive for social status during the reform decade, the *expectations* raised by the leadership for fundamental changes in this field have been even higher. In this way, the official propaganda has to bear part of the blame for the "diploma disease" harassing Chinese education.

Social Prestige
The Chinese have a tradition for respecting learned persons. An attempt was made to break down this respect during the Cultural Revolution, but after 1978 the intellectuals have been restored to an even higher position.

The term "intellectual" (*zhishi fenzi*) used to refer to anybody with at least a senior secondary education, but is now used more narrowly to refer to people with a college or specialized middle school diploma, and to people who do not have such an educational background, but who perform "mental" jobs, like for example school teachers. State and Party officials, on the other hand, who are engaged in administrative rather than academic work are normally referred to as cadres rather than intellectuals. The intellectuals are thus a very heterogenous group ranging from top level scientists to village school teachers. All these different groups of intellectuals, but in particular scientists, have become the heroes of the reform decade, and have been praised in newspaper articles, novels and films as a most important element in China's modernization process. Although official propaganda continuously have emphasized that great contributions to China's development can be made in all jobs, the young generation soon understood the only thinly masked message that formal education had become the key to honour and glory.

Surveys have been made of Chinese middle school students' desires for future occupation,[1] and they unanimously show that the large majority of children, regardless of whether they are in junior or senior middle schools, "key" or ordinary schools, or from urban or rural areas want to become doctors, scientists and engineers, in short, to join one of the professions demanding some sort of higher education. As only a few percent of an age group can achieve this goal, their ambitions are most often disappointed. The contradiction between ambitions and genuine prospects is most pronounced in rural areas, where practically no children want to become peasants, although this is what most of them will end up being. Though the hard and often dull life of a Chinese peasant has never attracted young people, the distaste for rural life has never been stronger than during the 1980s, and it has never been more socially acceptable to express one's ambition of leaving the countryside. A national survey of peasant families showed that this ambition is shared by the parents of the village youngsters. Almost 80% of all parents hoped that their children would be able to go to either a university (67%) or a specialized middle school, and 90% hoped for their children that they would be able to leave the countryside.[2] This has, of course, created an enormous pressure on the educational system, given that an academic or technical education is almost the only way to get a job, and thereby a residence permit, in a city.

Another reflection of the new social ranking of occupations is the preference of young people looking for a spouse. When the first marriage bureaus opened around 1980, one of their problems was that working class girls tried to avoid marrying other workers. They wanted to be introduced to intellectuals instead, because the latter were supposed to live a more interesting and cultivated life. In order to show that culture could exist even outside the ranks of intellectuals, one of the magazines which mentioned the problem found a model example of a female school teacher who had chosen a worker as her husband and was now living a culturally rich life with him. He even read Shakespeare and Victor Hugo, we were told, and was (in spite, it seems, of his humble social status) a very polite and pleasant person.[3] The increased social prestige of intellectuals has been accompanied by a rise in their own self-esteem and has led to a situation where working with one's brains rather than with one's hands has again become a source of pride.

---

1. Some of these surveys have been translated into English in *CE*, vol. 17, no. 4, winter 1984-85.

2. *Nongye jingji wenti* (Problems in Agricultural Economy) no. 8, 1988, pp. 45-51.

3. *ZGQN* no. 3, 1981, pp. 20-21.

Political status

The reform leaders have also made an attempt to make education the key to political influence. The liberalization of the academic and political climate has given intellectuals more opportunities to leave their mark on the public debate, and a number of high level intellectuals have worked in the think-tanks of political leaders, where they have directly influenced the political process.

Influential figures like Hu Yaobang, Party leader from 1981 to 1987, repeatedly stressed the important political role of the intellectuals and advocated the raising of the educational profile of Party members.[4] Intellectuals in China have traditionally had a low degree of representation in the Party, particularly compared to the Soviet Union and Eastern Europe. Only 4% of the Party members had a college background in 1984, and only 13.8% were graduates from senior or specialized middle schools, while more than 42% had received only primary school education and 10% were illiterates.[5] The reformers have tried to change this pattern. According to a *Hong Qi* (*Red Flag*) article, the proportion of "specialized technical personnel" (a term used synonymously with "intellectuals" in the article) among new Party recruits went up from 8.3% in 1978 to 27% in 1983 and to around 40% in the first half of 1984.[6] Several reports in the press show, however, that many Party officials have been reluctant to recruit large numbers of intellectuals into the Party and consequently have obstructed the process in a number of ways because they did not see intellectuals as valid members of the working class.[7]

The Party's attention has not only been directed towards those who already have a university degree. Students in universities and specialized middle schools are, in the words of one Party report on the recruitment question "...the reserve forces in the intellectual ranks. We must vigorously strengthen our work of recruiting Party members among them".[8] Students, however, primarily join the Communist Youth League, which recruits a much larger proportion of students than of other groups. In 1981, for example, 86% of the new university students

---

4. See for example his "Report at the Meeting in Commemoration of the Centenary of the Death of Karl Marx", translated in *BR* no. 12, 1983, pp. I-XV.

5. SWB/FE/7905/BII/1-2 (21 Mar 85).

6. *Hong Qi* (*Red Flag*) no. 23, 1984, p. 16-18.

7. SWB/FE/7905/BII/1-2 (21 Mar 85).

8. Ibid.

were League members,[9] and most of the remaining students join the League after their enrolment. This partly reflects students' own ambitions, as they know that League membership is good for their educational career, but it is also the result of a conscious recruitment policy by the Party.

Party and League membership is not in itself an accurate measure of political status, as the Party is a hierarchic organization, where grassroot members have only limited influence. There has, however, also been a strong movement to make formal education the key to joining the political and administrative elite: the cadre corps. According to the official plan half of the cadres by 1990 shall be university graduates, while the other half shall have reached the senior secondary level.[10] Some progress has definitely been made in this direction. In 1987, 25% of the cadres had a college background against 18% in 1980; 48% had a senior secondary education against 42% in 1980, while the proportion of those with only junior secondary education had fallen from 40% in 1980 to 27% in 1987.[11] By 1989 the proportion of cadres with a college background had risen to 28%.[12] Though the change may seem rather moderate, it should be kept in mind that the most important Party policy for the young generation of intellectuals is the recruitment pattern for new cadres. Over 60% of the young cadres promoted to leading posts at and above county level by the end of 1984 had received at least college education.[13] The Party spokesman who gave this figure stressed that not only the formal level of education but also the "actual performance" of the cadres should be considered; nevertheless it seems safe to conclude that the reform wing has been successful in changing the recruitment pattern of high level cadres to the advantage of college graduates and persons who have reached a similar professional level through self study. At the absolute top level, we find that 12 out of 18 members of the CCP Politbureau in 1987 had a college background compared to nine out of 28 in 1982 and only six out of 26 in 1977.[14]

There are, however, limits to how far the Party has been willing to go in its upgrading of the intellectuals' political status. While intellectual protagonists

9. *Zhongguo Baike Nianjian 1982*, p. 573.

10. *BR* no. 14, 1984, p. 24.

11. SWB/FE/0181 B2/3 (18 Jun 88).

12. SWB/FE/0566 B2/5 (20 Sep 89).

13. SWB/FE/8151/BII/4 (7 Jan 86).

14. *Li and White 1988*, p. 379.

in Chinese literary works, including those of Wang Meng, Minister of Culture up to 1989, have often been portrayed as the leading force in the modernization process, the same point cannot be openly stated in official circles. When Fang Lizhi was expelled from the Party and dismissed from his post as vice-president of the Chinese Science and Technology University in January, 1987, one of the accusations against him was exactly that he had disseminated "the so-called theory that intellectuals are the dominant factor" and encouraged Chinese intellectuals to "show their strength".[15] This was obviously beyond the limits of what the Party, as "vanguard of the proletariat", was willing to accept even before June, 1989.

Job Opportunities

Education has also gained importance for a person's job opportunities. One example of this is the armed forces, which after 1949 became an important ladder of upward social mobility for young peasants, to whom it gave a professional and political training enabling them to either become officers or take up leading positions in their native villages after demobilization. During the reform years, however, the modernization of the army has reduced the need for huge numbers of often poorly educated recruits from the villages, and the new generation of officers have won their positions in examination halls rather than on the battlefield or at political meetings. In the air force, for example, 62% of the cadres in the "leading organizations" in 1984 were college educated, and the report mentioning this figure writes, almost in a tone of pity, about the old generation of army cadres who "came from workers' and peasants' families, and were often poorly educated".[16]

Other trades have been professionalized in a similar way. Lawyers have been trained to take over the judicial sector from the politically appointed cadres. Formally trained medical doctors have become the focus of attention rather than the "barefoot doctors" of the Cultural Revolution decade. In the industrial sector formal education has become more and more important in the selection of managers and other administrative staff, and it has even become necessary for the older generation of managers to go back to school in order to raise their formal educational level. From 1983 to early 1988 as many as 176,000 managers of industrial enterprises took national examinations in management related fields.[17]

---

15. SWB/FE/8471/BII/2-4 (21 Jan 87) and 8472/BII/5-7 (22 Jan 87).

16. SWB/FE/7767/BII/8 (6 Oct 84).

17. SWB/FE/0046 B2/6 (12 Jan 88).

It has likewise been the policy of the central leaders to demand that workers and other employees go through relevant training before getting a job. This principle of "first training, then job" (*xian peixun, hou jiuye*), which is crucial for the success of the vocationalization of secondary education, is part of the general move towards greater emphasis on formal training received inside the school system. It has been very difficult to implement, however. Because of the higher prestige attached to general education many enterprises have prefered to recruit their workers through examinations in general school subjects rather than considering the vocational training of the applicants. Other enterprises have resisted the pressure for reforms and still hire workers according to non-meritocratic criteria, for example through family connections.

At the bottom of the socio-economic hierarchy, lack of education greatly increases the risk of becoming unemployed. A 1987 survey in Shandong province, for example, demonstrated that 63% of all rural jobless people between the age of 15 and 18 were either illiterate or had attended only primary school, and that this was the case for three-quarters of the jobless girls.[18]

While education has become more important for job opportunities at all levels of the public sector, alternative roads to wealth have been opened in the newly emerged private sector where formal education plays a rather limited role. Economic liberalization has created a group of "entrepreneurs" in rural as well as urban areas whose success and failure are based more on ability and luck than on academic diplomas. In the beginning of the reform period these people often came from the fringes of society and held little public respect. In later years, however, even college and graduate students have dropped out of school in order to go into business.

Income and Living Conditions

Though more jobs now demand a college or specialized middle school education, the material benefits connected to these jobs are still very limited. It has been the official policy that "...intellectuals' pay should be raised. Comrades who use their knowledge to help the country and people become affluent as quickly as possible must be generously awarded".[19] Some pay rises have been given, for example to school teachers, but they have quickly been eaten up by inflation, and Chinese newspapers and magazines have abounded with complaints over the low wages and poor living standards of intellectuals. Remarks like: "Those who make

---

18. SWB/FE/0148 B2/3 (11 May 88).

19. SWB/FE/7874/BII/6 (13 Feb 85).

atomic bombs are paid less than those who sell eggs; those who hold scalpels are paid less than those who hold barber's razors" have been put forward at official meetings,[20] and the 1988 Chinese People's Political Consultative Conference was even told that "the average age of the intellectuals who died in recent years was 51, compared with the national average of 68".[21] Statements of this type should, of course, be regarded as part of the intellectuals' fight to get a bigger piece of the cake, and they are often difficult to verify, but it does seem that the intellectuals' incomes have not kept pace with the advantages gained by workers and peasants through the bonus and contract systems. Some village school teachers, for example, have been impoverished to such a degree that they have left their teaching positions in order to take up farming or go into business,[22] and in October, 1988, the State Statistical Bureau published the results of a survey which showed that the average monthly income of "mental workers" in Beijing was only 172 *yuan* compared to 182 *yuan* for "manual workers".[23]

Conclusion

The high social status attached to education in China during the reform decade has only partly been rooted in material reality. The living standard of Chinese intellectuals has not improved dramatically, and many, typically the school teachers, live under very poor conditions indeed. The educational profile of the Party and of the cadre corps has been raised, but only gradually and changes have not made themselves felt until the last part of the 1980s. Social prestige has, perhaps, been the greatest advantage of a high level of formal education.

The traditional high status of education in China, however, and the constant promises of the political leadership to strengthen the role of the educated in the reform process, was enough to create a storm on the best secondary schools. For most young people no alternative career paths were within reach. Connections to influential people (*guanxi*) could be one possibility, but such connections are difficult to obtain if one's family does not have them already. The life of the entrepreneurs is economically risky and vulnerable to policy changes. Though the

---

20. SWB/FE/0149 B2/1 (12 May 88).

21. SWB/FE/0117/i (5 Apr 88).

22. 300,000 primary and middle school teachers are reported to have left their jobs "in recent times" because of low wages, SWB/FE/0256 B2/7 (14 Sep 88). See also *CE* vol. 20, no. 1, spring 1987, for a translation of several reports and surveys discussing the living standard and work conditions of Chinese intellectuals.

23. *GMRB*, 6 October, 1988, p. 1.

chance of getting ahead through the educational system has been a rather slim one, it has for most young people been the only available channel.

The concern of the Chinese for their children's future have made them give high priority to educational issues, and the leaders must therefore consider the educational demands of different social groups on a par with demands for material progress. Thus, educational reforms have not only been a matter of matching the qualifications transmitted in school with the needs of Chinese society and finding the right jobs to the right people, but also a question of social distribution.

In Chapters 2 through 4, we have examined the larger context in which the reforms of secondary education have taken place: The historical experiences with different strategies for secondary education, the main ideological and political trends in the reform period and the importance of secondary education for social status. In the following chapters we shall turn to the formulation and implementation of the secondary educational reform policies and their effects on Chinese society.

5. A General Outline of Chinese Secondary Education in the Reform Period

This chapter will outline the structure, aims, curriculum and funding of Chinese secondary education during the reform decade. This general level presentation will serve as a frame of reference for the discussion in Chapters 6 to 10 of a number of specific aspects of the reforms.

Structure

The structure of the Chinese educational system as it looks in most localities in the late 1980s is shown in Table 5.1. This structure has, however, been subject to a number of changes during the reform period, and local experiments are still carried out with other models.

In the present structure, students attend six years of primary school, three years of junior secondary and three years of senior secondary school (6+3+3). This is in accordance with the main tendency in the period from 1953 up to the Cultural Revolution. After the re-opening of schools in the late 1960s however, the period of schooling was shortened to either nine (5+2+2) or ten (5+3+2) years. In the short run, the latter structure survived the fall of the "Gang of Four" and became formalized through the enacting of the "Draft Instructional Plan for Ten Years Full Time Secondary and Primary Schools" in January, 1978.

In September, 1980 however, Shanghai, Beijing and some other localities decided to extend the period of schooling by one year. Shanghai wanted to add a year to senior secondary school from 1981, while Beijing would extend primary school to six years.[1] In October the CCP decided that urban but not rural areas could extend primary school by one year,[2] and in December it committed itself in principle to the 6+3+3 structure.[3] In March 1981, the Ministry stressed that the level of education for graduates of six-year primary schools should "in

---

1. *Jiaoyu Dashiji*, entry 80108, pp. 592-3.

2. *Jiaoyu Dashiji*, entry 80121, p. 595.

3. See "Zhonggong zhongyang, Guowuyuan guanyu puji xiaoxue ruogan wenti de jueding" (Decision of the CCP Central Committee and the State Council on Certain Questions Concerning the Popularization of Primary Education). In *Jiaoyu Gaige*, pp. 403-408.

principle" be the same as for those who had gone through the five-year course.[4] Though it is evident that this would not be the case in real life, the Ministry wanted to keep up the illusion that all students would compete on an equal footing for a place in the best middle schools, which had begun to enroll students through competitive examinations.

In April, 1981, a "Draft Instructional Plan for Full Time Six Years Key Middle Schools" was issued. The extension of senior secondary school from two to three years was intended to start with the key schools. The principle of identity in content between the two-year and the three-year senior secondary programs was upheld in the beginning. In 1983, however, it was decided to introduce two different sets of curricula, a full one for the key schools and other schools of good quality following the three-year program, and a reduced one for two-year courses and three year courses in low quality schools.[5] During the 1980s, the 6+3+3 system gradually spread, first to non-key schools in the cities, later also to rural areas. It is still not universal, however, as some of the less developed rural areas are still only able to offer five years of primary education.[6] Even in areas which now have the twelve-year system, it will not be before some time in the 1990s that it can be taken for granted that a senior secondary school graduate has attended twelve years of schooling.

The discussion of whether the 6+3+3 structure is ideal for all parts of China is not finished yet. The most important alternative is a structure of five years primary school followed by four years junior and three years senior secondary education (5+4+3). The main argument for this model is that the curriculum of junior secondary school is too extensive to cover in only three years, particularly as it now in some places should include vocational subjects along with the traditional academic ones. The primary school curriculum, on the other hand, can allegedly be finished in five years without major difficulties.[7] The 5+4+3 model has been implemented on a trial basis in some top quality schools, like the Jingshan school in Beijing. It has also become popular in some rural areas, however, where the large majority of junior secondary school graduates leave school, and where the fourth year is therefore needed for the teaching of vocational subjects. The results in both types of schools are reported

---

4. *Jaioyu Dashiji*, entry 8129, p. 611.

5. *Zhongguo Jiaoyu Nianjian 1982-1984*, p. 86.

6. For example Ningxia Province, cf. *JYYJ* no. 8, 1987, pp. 50-54. This survey clearly brings out the difficulties facing education in the less developed parts of China.

7. See for example *JYYJ* no. 8, 1986, pp. 6-7.

to be excellent.[8] The 5+4+3 model may gain some ground in the future, but the lack of qualified middle school teachers will probably inhibit its general implementation.

Another important structural change has been the diversification of senior secondary education. Vocational and agricultural middle schools have been established on a large scale, and students in specialized middle schools and workers' training schools, who up to the mid-1980s often were recruited among general senior middle school graduates now normally come directly from the junior section (cf. Chapter 8).

Aims

Officially, secondary education has the "double task" (*shuangchong renwu*) of "providing the higher level of schools with qualified students and training a fine labour reserve force for society".[9] This formula, however, is a manifestation of the inherent dilemma in the system rather than a guideline, because it is unclear whether *all* schools should train *all* students with this aim, or whether a certain division of work should take place. Up to 1978 Chinese secondary education was, in principle, a comprehensive system, which was not expected to decide the future occupation of the students. The establishment of the key schools changed this situation because these schools obviously emphasized college preparation, but in theory the "double task" principle survived.

The vocationalization of almost half of all senior secondary schools during the 1980s represented a further division of work among different types of middle schools. Even with only half of all senior secondary school students in the academic track, however, most of them are still unable to continue their education after graduation and are forced to find a job for which they have received no specific training. This contradiction has led to a discussion of the meaning and even the relevance of the "double task" concept. Some debaters have suggested that enrolment in general senior secondary school should be reduced considerably and that these schools should then concentrate on the preparation of future college students.[10] This would reduce the pressure on tertiary education, because fewer students would be turned down at the entrance examinations, increase the role of vocational education and, implicitly, relieve general schools of the obligation to

---

8. *JYYJ* no. 6, 1988, pp. 15-18.

9. *Zhongguo Jiaoyu Nianjian 1949-1981*, p. 147.

10. See for example *JYYJ* no. 9, 1985 pp. 14-16 (English translation in *CE,* vol. 20, no. 4, pp. 87-98) and *JYYJ* no. 2, 1988, pp. 21-25.

offer vocational and labour courses. It would also free some of the resources now spent on vocational training for middle school students *after* graduation. So far, the "double task" principle still seems to stand its ground at least at the verbal level, since a rigid selection of students after junior middle school would have even worse consequences than the current system.[11]

The "double task" principle defines the obligations of secondary education towards society. In relation to the students, it is the aim of secondary school to imbue them with patriotism, communist ethics and a proletarian world view and outlook toward life. It shall further make them serve the people, provide them with basic knowledge and skills, develop their abilities and intellect and take care of their health and mental development. Finally it shall give them some ideas about aesthetic judgment and some labour skills.[12] Both ideological and technical qualifications are thus emphasized, and the phrasing is in accordance with the traditional "red and expert" ideal. We shall return to the concrete implementation of these principles in the subsequent chapters.

Curriculum

The control over the content of secondary education has become more centralized during the reforms. Instructional plans and curriculum guidelines are centrally decided by the State Education Commission (before 1985 the Ministry of Education), and teaching materials are nationally standardized. During the Cultural Revolution decade, the lower administrative levels had more control over what was taught in the schools, and the production of locally relevant materials was encouraged.

According to the 1981 instructional plan, Chinese middle school students attend classes for thirty four (junior) or thirty two (senior) weeks a year. Exams take up four weeks plus an extra couple of weeks for final examinations after the last year of both the junior and senior sections. The time spent on manual labour is two weeks in junior and four weeks in senior middle school. Winter and summer vacations take up the remaining ten to eleven weeks.[13]

Table 5.2 shows the number of weekly lessons allocated to each subject according to the 1981 plan. This plan was designed primarily for the key schools and other schools who wanted their students to compete for access to university,

---

11. For a summary of the first phase of the discussion on the "double task" see *JYYJ* no. 10, 1986, pp. 36-42, particularly pp. 41-42.

12. *Zhongguo Jiaoyu Nianjian 1949-1981*, p. 147.

13. *Zhongguo Jiaoyu Nianjian 1949-1981*, p. 158.

and the provinces were allowed to find less ambitious solutions for schools of lower quality. However, as the university entrance examinations were based on this curriculum and as the pressure on the schools to qualify their students for this examination was very strong, practically all schools tried to follow it as closely as possible.

Deviations have tended to give even more emphasis to college preparation. For example, many schools have divided their senior secondary students into a "science" and a "culture" stream to match the parallel division of the university entrance examination.[14] Furthermore, the number of lessons has been increased in many schools, sometimes up to as many as forty a week, because the curriculum guidelines are so ambitious that it is very difficult to cover the full content inside the allotted time.[15] Other schools try to solve this problem by concentrating exclusively on the subjects tested in the university entrance examination at the expense of subjects like history and geography.

Some rural schools, realizing that their students' chances for gaining admission to university are minimal, drop the foreign language classes, partly because they do not have qualified teachers for them, and partly because most rural students lack motivation to learn a foreign language. Others offer vocational classes to some or all students. Still, most schools follow a curriculum similar to the standard one, and the central authorities do their best to prevent deviations.

In connection with the "double task" discussion mentioned above, it should be noted that the curriculum has a high degree of subject specialization and that biology, which is of great potential value particularly for rural students, receives little attention. This indicates that the present system has been primarily designed to meet the needs of those who will continue on to college, while considerations about what types of knowledge and skills would be most useful for the majority of students who will join the agricultural or industrial work force have been of secondary importance.

---

14. In fact, this can hardly be called a deviation, as different timetables for these two tracks were included as an alternative in the 1981 instructional plan, cf. *Zhongguo Jiaoyu Nianjian 1949-1981*, p. 158.

15. Cf. *JYYJ* no. 9, 1989, pp. 65-70, where experiences with the 1981 instructional plan are summed up based on a case study of 25 middle schools in Jiangsu Province.

Funding

Education in China is financed through a variety of sources of which direct government support is still the most important. Table 5.3 shows how government investments in education have increased significantly in absolute figures during the reform period. Seen in relation to China's gross national product, national income and state expenditures however, the impressive increase in educational investments during the first years of the reform period has been followed by a certain stagnation from 1982 onwards, and China's educational expenses in proportion to gross national product only ranks 100th in the world.[16]

To these investments by the state come funds from other sources. According to preliminary statistics for 1987, educational institutions earned 2.67 billion *yuan* through productive activities, 2.64 billion were collected in education fees, enterprises invested two billion *yuan* in education, 1.62 billion came in through public fund raising (including contributions from overseas Chinese) and almost 1.6 billion came from other sources, most important of which were different kinds of extra fees paid by the students.[17] This all adds up to more than ten billion *yuan*, a significant figure when set alongside the 30 billion invested by the government. In 1982 the World Bank found that public expenditures covered 74% of all education expenditures in China,[18] and according to the figures quoted above this is still the case.

Secondary education received around 40% of the total expenditures on education in 1979 as well as in 1982,[19] and it seems to have maintained its share in recent years. Seen in the light of the general increase in educational investments this should mean that the economic conditions of Chinese middle schools have improved considerably during the reform period. This is not necessarily the case, however, and the reasons for this are many

First of all, a large proportion of the extra funds have been spent on raising the salaries of the teachers. While these pay rises have been important for upholding the quality of teaching by stopping teachers from quitting the teaching profession, it has also meant that 72.2% of all operating expenses went to salaries, pensions etc... in 1987 against 66.9% in 1980. The average annual expenditure per student in middle school for pedagogical purposes (including equip-

---

16. *BR* no. 29, 17-23 July, 1989, p. 21.

17. *ZGJYB*, August 18, 1988, p. 4.

18. *World Bank 1985*, pp. 46.

19. *World Bank 1985*, pp. 48.

ment) was thus still only five *yuan*.[20] Considering inflation, this means, at least according to some debaters, that the annual expenditure per student has actually been reduced.[21] Exactly how much educational investments have been and should be raised has been the object of much debate in China,[22] but it is, at least, quite obvious that the impressive increase in absolute figures is misleading.

Secondly, the financial situation of Chinese middle schools is far from uniform. While city schools, in particular key schools, receive considerable state support, almost all rural schools are funded by the local peasant community. The central government has taken great pains to explain to the peasants that though it issues detailed guidelines for what should be taught in all Chinese schools, it is only willing to finance urban and elite education. In February, 1984, Hebei was given much publicity as a model province for educational reform in the countryside. One of the newspaper articles praising the progress made in Hebei gave this summary of how the policy of local funding of education was explained to the peasants:

> Our country has two kinds of socialist ownership, public and collective. The salary of the workers of publicly owned enterprises is the labour income of the individual after the "six kinds of deduction" have been made (one of them being education fees). Therefore it is only fair that their health, education and pension expenses are covered by the state. The peasants working under the collective system are in a different position. Except for a modest agricultural tax, their labour incomes belong to the collective or to themselves. In this situation the cost of their children's education should be covered by the collective or by themselves, not by the state. Actually, the state does not cover their medical and pension expenditures, so why should it pay for the education of their children? ....[23]

That the financial responsibility for rural education rests with the local levels leads to a considerable difference in standard between provinces, counties and even villages. Though the standard of education not only depends on economic factors, Chinese researchers comparing richer and poorer counties have found a

20. *ZGJYB*, August 18, 1988, p. 4.

21. *JYYJ* no. 9, 1986, pp. 17-22, particularly p. 20.

22. Articles from this debate have been translated in *CE*, vol. 17, no. 3, fall 1984.

23. *GMRB*, Feb. 23, 1984, p. 1.

significant positive correlation between high per capita income level and the degree of universalization of education.[24]

Conclusion

In the course of the reforms, the combined length of primary and secondary education was extended from ten to twelve years in order to raise the quality of education. The term "quality" has been defined by the central educational bureaucracy in Beijing who have designed teaching plans and teaching materials for universal use all over China. In this way, an attempt has been made to standardize the qualifications transmitted to urban and rural students and to students living in areas at different levels of economic development. The curriculum has been arranged according to traditional academic disciplines with no consideration for the special needs of the rural areas.

The rural communities, on the other hand, cover the major part of the costs of local education, while urban and elite education is financed by the higher administrative units (cities, provinces and the state). This means that the rural areas have to pay for an education over which they have very limited control.[25]

We shall now turn to three fields where the post-Mao reforms of secondary education have broken radically with the policies of the Cultural Revolution decade: Enrolment policies (Chapter 6), selection criteria and methods (Chapter 7) and the relationship between education and the world of work (Chapter 8).

---

24. *JYYJ* no. 10, 1989, pp. 39-44.

25. For a more detailed look at the theme of centralization of control vs. decentralization of financial responsibility, see *Rosen 1985* and *Robinson 1986*.

6. Enrolment and Completion

This chapter will first discuss the effects of the post-Mao reforms in education on secondary school enrolment. Next, the changes in official enrolment policy and the 1986 law on nine years compulsory education will be taken up. Finally, the dropout problem and the reasons for the expansion of this phenomenon will be discussed. As mentioned in the preceding chapter, the effects of the reforms in the cities have not been identical with those in the countryside. The questions of enrolment and completion will therefore be related to the theme of urban/rural inequality.

Enrolment

A highly conspicuous change in post-Mao secondary education, which has received very little attention in the Chinese debate, has been the dramatic cutback in enrolment. Table 6.1 shows how the number of students in the junior section fell from almost 50 million in the peak years of 1977 and 1978 to less than 37 million in 1983.[1] Since that time, enrolment has slowly risen again to a level around 41 million. The number of students in the senior section was cut in half between the late 1970s and 1983, but it too has been increasing since 1983. General senior middle schools have lost most ground because it has been the declared policy of the government to transfer students at this level from general to vocational schools (cf. Chapter 8). The growth in the number of students after 1983 is due to the larger enrolment in vocational schools and to the extension of senior middle school from two to three years.

During the reform decade a decreasing proportion of primary school graduates have continued on to junior middle school (cf. Table 6.2). Up through the 1970s, around 90% of primary school graduates enrolled in junior middle school each year. This proportion has dropped to around 70% in the 1980s. It should be noted that children leaving primary school in 1987 had normally received one more year of schooling than their counterparts of the 1970s. But in rural areas, where most of the early school leavers are to be found, the extension

---

1. Sources are found in the notes for the tables. The quality of official Chinese statistics has been much improved in the 1980s, though they are still not without problems. For a discussion of these problems see *Henze 1987*.

of primary school from five to six years has only been effective in the last few years included in the table, so there is still a very large number of students who have left the educational system after only five years in school. With regard to the entrance rate to secondary school, China only ranks 80th among 139 countries in the world.[2]

The transition rate to senior middle school was abnormally high (60-70%) in the years from 1975 to 1977. After 1978 it returned to the 40% level of the early 1970s, but then dropped further to 34% in 1988. This decrease is even more significant seen in the light of the drop in the number of junior middle school graduates from almost 17 million in 1977 to just above 11 million in 1988.

The consequence of the reduced enrolment is that a rising proportion of the young generation has left school without completing either junior or senior secondary school. The age groups born each year between 1963 and 1974 are quite similar in size, between 23 and 28 million per year with an average of just under 26 million.[3] These year groups should have entered junior middle school between 1975 and 1986, have graduated between 1978 and 1989 and entered senior middle school in those same years. The 23 million students enrolled in junior middle school in the years of 1976 and 1977 thus made up between 85% and 90% of their age group, while the more than 13 million students enrolled each year between 1982 and 1986 made up only around 50% of theirs. As only between 60% and 86% of junior middle school entrants in the 1980s completed the whole three year course (cf. Table 6.6), only 30% to 40% of the "reform generation" have completed junior middle school. Moving further up the ladder, only around 40% of the junior middle school graduates enrolled in any kind of senior middle school, which means that only 12% to 16% of the whole age group received any education at this level. These calculations are not without a factor of uncertainty, but they correspond very well with the World Bank estimates which state that junior middle schools enrolled only 46% of the relevant age group in 1983 against 63% in 1979, while the senior section enrolled 16% in 1983 against 36% in 1979.[4] According to the State Education Commission, only 53% of the relevant age group received junior secondary education in 1986,

---

2. *BR* no. 29, 17-23 July, 1989, p. 21.

3. *Census 1982*, p. 264-65.

4. *World Bank 1985*, p. 7-8.

while 13% attended senior middle school.[5] The extra years added to primary and senior secondary school since 1981 only make up for a small part of this loss.

The reduction in enrolment has been much heavier in rural than in urban areas (cf. Table 6.3). Still, Chinese secondary education has considerably less urban bias than before the Cultural Revolution. This is particularly true for the junior section, where the rural schools have lost relatively little ground over the last ten years, and then only to the town and county seat schools, which also enroll some of the children from the villages. In the senior section, however, urban schools enrolled almost 30% of all students in 1988 compared to less than 20% in 1977. While enrolment in urban schools has been cut by only 37% during these eleven years, the reduction in the two other groups put together has been 64%. Table 6.3 also brings out the strong tendency to concentrate senior secondary education in the county seats and towns instead of spreading it out to the villages. This has forced rural youths to become boarding students, thus increasing the financial burden on their families.

The data in Table 6.3 cover only general schools, but up to 1984 vocational schools held only a rather small share of the total enrolment. Furthermore, the primarily urban vocational middle schools have enrolled as many students as the agricultural schools of the rural areas up through the 1980s (cf. Table 8.1). Therefore, the inclusion of data from vocational schools would not change the picture radically.

Because of the traditional sceptical attitude to women's education in China, the decrease in total enrolment could be expected to lead to an even smaller representation of female students in middle school. Table 6.4 shows, however, that the proportion of female students in primary and secondary school has been stable over the last fifteen years after a significant rise during the Cultural Revolution decade. The girls still make up around 45% of primary school students and just above 40% of the students in general middle school. In the vocational schools they have even increased their share of the places to 44%. An important reason for the relatively strong position of the girls is probably that they do well on the entrance examinations to junior middle school because they are more mature than boys of the same age.

Enrolment Policy
During the first two years after the downfall of the Cultural Revolution leaders, the new top Party leadership had certain disagreements about the scale of enrol-

---

5. *RMJY* no. 11, 1986, p. 21.

ment. Deng Xiaoping constantly stressed the necessity of improving the quality of education, a phrase historically associated with an elite strategy leading to reduced enrolment.[6] Hua Guofeng, on the other hand, maintained that China should "develop all kinds and all levels of education on a larger scale and at a higher speed",[7] a phrase that corresponded with his extremely ambitious version of the "Four Modernizations" program. Nothing was said about reducing enrolment at this time. On the contrary, in late 1977 Fang Yi, member of the CCP politbureau and vice-president of the Chinese Academy of Sciences, insisted that China universalize senior secondary education in the cities and junior secondary education in the countryside before 1985.[8] At the national education conference in April 1978, Minister of Education Liu Xiyao restated these goals, though without a specific time limit.[9] This meant, if taken at face value, that the new leaders would continue the expansive enrolment policy of the Cultural Revolution decade.

After the balance of power changed to the advantage of Deng Xiaoping and the reform wing during 1978, Hua Guofeng's ambitious plans were set aside, and guidelines were issued ordering a cutback in enrolment.[10] Though there was some local opposition to this change in policy,[11] its implementation was almost immediately effected (cf. Table 6.1).

The main argument for the cutback was that the quality of the existing schools was too low because the Cultural Revolution enrolment expansion had overstrained China's human and material resources. The argumentation put forward in a 1979 *Guangming Daily* article describing the situation in Guangdong was typical in this respect. It documented the enormous expansion in middle school enrolment in the 1970s and found that it had left Guangdong secondary schools with a number of serious problems: The number of qualified teachers was insufficient, and there was a shortage of money, buildings and equipment. There-

---

6. See, for example, Deng's speech at the National Conference on Education on April 22, 1978. In *Deng 1984*, pp. 119-126.

7. *Jiaoyu Dashiji*, entry 7721, p. 495.

8. Said at a meeting on 27 December, 1977. *Jiaoyu Dashiji*, entry 7763, p. 504.

9. Liu's speech is translated in *CE*, vol. 12, no. 1, 1979, p. 15 ff.

10. Suzanne Pepper has discussed the consequences of the cutback in different provinces in *Pepper 1984*, p. 13-19.

11. Ibid.

fore, the academic level of the students had dropped.[12] The same report also mentioned that the post-Mao cutback in enrolment had provoked protests. These had mainly come from the cities and from densely populated areas, where there was no use for extra unskilled manpower. Parents in such areas preferred to keep their sons and daughters in school, even if the quality of education was low, because they did not feel the children had other options. The report expressed understanding for these worries but found that this was a social problem which the educational system could not shoulder alone.

During the early 1980s serious flaws in the elite strategy became more and more apparent (cf. Chapter 7), and so did the question of education in the rural areas. In May 1983 the Party Central Committee and the State Council jointly issued a "Message on Certain Questions in the Strengthening and Reform of Rural Education" which called for the universalization of primary education in rural areas before the year 1990. The "Message" emphasized, however, that in the most remote areas this goal could not be reached, and that in other places it would only be possible to run half-time schools or offer the most essential courses. In accordance with this realistic attitude to the state of rural education the "Message" demanded that only the richest and most developed areas should begin to universalize junior secondary education, while the majority should still concentrate on raising the quality of the existing junior secondary schools.[13]

Two years later, however, in May 1985, a much more ambitious plan was presented in the form of the Central Committee's "Decision on the Reform of the Educational System". This "Decision", which was intended to be the "master plan" for all future work in the field of education, called for the step by step implementation of a system of nine years compulsory education. The economically developed areas, mostly the cities and the coastal provinces, were to universalize junior secondary education before 1990. Such areas were said to hold one quarter of China's population. Areas at the middle level of development, comprising half of the total population, were to achieve the same goal around 1995. The last quarter of the population was said to live in economically backward areas, and they were to work in the same direction but with no specific time limit.[14] In his presentation of the "Decision", vice premier Wan Li admitted that the plan would be extremely difficult to implement, and that "some com-

---

12. *GMRB*, 20 May, 1979, p.1-2.

13. "Zhonggong zhongyang, Guowuyuan guanyu jiaqiang he gaige nongcun xuexiao jiaoyu ruogan wenti de tongzhi". In *Jiaoyu Gaige*, pp 471-476.

14. "Zhonggong zhongyang guanyu jiaoyu tizhi gaige de jueding". In *Jiaoyu Gaige*, pp. 15-28.

rades" were quite sceptical and felt that the call for a universalization of junior middle school was premature.[15]

The law on nine years compulsory education was passed by the National People's Congress in April, 1986, officially making it China's aim to universalize junior secondary school during the 1990s. There is still some ambiguity on this point however. In the official presentation of the new instructional plans for the nine years of compulsory education, for example, a different vision of the future scale of enrolment is offered:

> Graduates from primary and middle school will go through three streaming processes. The first time will be when they graduate from primary school, when two thirds will continue to junior middle school, while one third must prepare themselves for taking part in productive labour. The second time is after junior middle school, when around one fifth of the graduates will go on to general senior middle school, another fifth to other types of senior middle schools, while the last three fifths will take part in work or labour. The third time is after graduation from general senior middle school, when one fourth will continue on to higher education while three fourths will take part in work or labour.[16]

The authorities thus only expect two thirds of the primary school graduates (less than 60% of the age group) to start in junior middle school in the 1990s. This makes the law on nine years compulsory education a symbolic political act intended to satisfy the popular concern for primary and junior secondary education, rather than an actual enrolment plan.

The Dropout Problem
The fact that a decreasing share of the relevant age group has been attending middle school in the 1980s is only partly due to the priority given to the "raising of standards" (tigao) at the cost of "popularization" (puji) and the subsequent decision to cut down on enrolment. Another important reason is the dropout problem, which has been recognized by the government as very serious, particularly at the junior middle school level.

---

15. Wan Li: "Zai quanguo jiaoyu gongzuo huiyishang de jianghua" (Speech at the National Education Work Conference) (27 May, 1985). In *Jiaoyu Gaige*, pp. 33-46.

16. *RMJY* no. 12, 1986, p. 16-18.

Table 6.5 shows the dimensions of the problem. The completion rate for junior middle school students was very high up to 1978.[17] During the next few years, however, when tests and examinations had again become very important and the full attention of the authorities was focused on elite education (cf. Chapter 7), the completion rate dropped so quickly that it is appropriate to talk about a breakdown in junior secondary education. Schools were closed and millions of students were sent home in the effort to "raise the quality" of secondary education. Since the early 1980s the system has begun to recover, though many students are still being lost during the three years. The most massive dropout occurs during the second year of junior middle school. According to World Bank figures for the years 1979-1983, 12% of all students dropped out between grades one and two and 22% between grades two and three.[18]

The gradual extension of senior middle school from two to three years makes it impossible to calculate dropout rates in the same way as in Table 6.5. According to an official Chinese source, however, the problem has now become quite serious at this level, too. In 1988 a moderate 2.2% of the general senior middle school students dropped out, but in agricultural and vocational middle schools the proportion was as high as 8.8%, which means that only around three fourths of the entrants complete the three-year course.[19]

Around 1978-79, when the dropout problem was most serious, everyone in the educational system was so engrossed in the discussion of how to implement the new examination and elite school system that the exodus of millions of middle school students passed almost unnoticed. Up through the 1980s more attention has been paid to the problem, which according to reports has been most acute in the countryside. A Chinese survey of a rather wealthy county in Heilongjiang Province demonstrates the extent of the problem. This county had universalized primary education, but only 40% of its primary school leavers continued their education in junior middle school. Among these students the dropout rate rose dramatically after 1978. During the Cultural Revolution the dropout rate had been only slightly above 20%. Of the 1979 entrants, however, 44% did not graduate three years later. For the next year of students the dropout rate went up to 67%, and of the students entering middle school in 1981 as many as 72% had dropped

17. Because some junior middle schools had only a two year curriculum in the mid-1970s, these years are not included in the table. Data from these years (cf. same source as Table 6.5) show, however, that the completion rates were as high as for the 1975-78 students.

18. *World Bank 1985*, p. 8.

19. *BR* no. 29, 17-23 July, 1989, p. 22.

out before 1984.[20] Several reports from other provinces have spoken of dropout rates from rural junior middle schools of around 50%,[21] and rates of 40-50% have been admitted to be quite common for whole districts (including towns).[22] Some areas are thus hit much harder than national statistics indicate.

In 1989, the dropout problem received renewed attention after it turned out that 6.9% of all junior middle school students dropped out in 1988. If this trend is not reversed, the completion rate will again drop below the 80% level. The State Education Commission now threatens that "local government and education officials who fail to reduce the dropout rate will be dealt with for dereliction of duty".[23] The effect of such threats remains to be seen.

The most often heard explanation for the alarming dropout rates is the influence of the contract system in agriculture, which makes it attractive for peasant households to withdraw their children from school so that they can work on the family land or look after younger children. This is, for example, how the World Bank explains the decrease in students' attendance rates in rural areas.[24] The use of child labour in industry has also increased and millions of children of school age have left school before graduation in order to work in industry or agriculture. The problem is most serious in rural areas with a developed commodity economy, where children without a middle school certificate easily find jobs in small scale rural industry and in the commerce, service and transport sectors.[25] Another reason why many children leave school is that tuition fees have gone up. Together with expenses for books etc..., they can sometimes add up to as much as 100 *yuan* per semester,[26] which is a sum of money that many households simply cannot afford. Finally, the reduced number of village schools has meant longer distances between home and school, and this undoubtedly also has some effect on school attendance.

These objective reasons are no doubt important, but problems intrinsic to the school system itself should not be overlooked. The Heilongjiang survey

---

20. *JYYJ* no. 8, 1985, pp. 22, 33-36.

21. *JYYJ* no. 10, 1986, pp. 17-23; *RMJY* no. 11, 1986, p. 9; *ZGJYB*, May 21, 1987, p. 2.

22. *RMJY* no. 5, 1987, p. 2.

23. SWB/FE 0388 B2/3 (18 Feb 89).

24. *World Bank 1985*, p. i-ii.

25. *JYYJ* no. 10, 1989, pp. 49-53. This article contains an interesting presentation of the results of several Chinese surveys of the dropout problem.

26. SWB/FE/0397 B2/2, (1 Mar 89).

mentioned above found that the contract system only bore a small part of the blame for the high dropout rates, as most families in the area under survey already had ample labour power. The reason, according to the survey, was rather to be found inside the schools, where teachers concentrated only on the students who had a chance of passing the entrance examination to senior secondary school and ignored the rest (we shall return to this problem in Chapter 7). The same trend was found in a Hunan survey, which claimed that teacher neglect and lack of motivation for study due to low marks accounted for 55% of all dropout cases in the schools surveyed.[27]

Conclusion
The statistical data show how the reform decade has been a period of recession for secondary education in terms of enrolment and completion. There has been a significant decrease in the number of senior secondary school students, not only in the general stream but also in the total figure for all types of schools. The number of students in junior secondary school has also dropped, in absolute figures as well as in proportion to the age group. Even after the enactment of the law on nine years compulsory education, the authorities estimate that only two thirds of all primary school graduates will continue on to junior middle school. If we assume, very optimistically, that 90% of each year group will complete primary education, this still means that only 60% of a total year group will enter junior middle school. Given the present junior middle school completion rate of around 80%, less than half of the relevant age group will thus receive the "compulsory" nine years of education in the future. During the reform decade the rate of children who have received eight or nine years of schooling has been as far down as 30 to 40%. The universalization of nine years of education in China is therefore still a very remote objective.

The decrease in the number of middle school students has partly been due to central policies aiming at closing down low quality schools established during the Cultural Revolution decade. As most of these schools were located in the countryside, the closures have been most visible here. Changes in agricultural policy making it more attractive to use child labour have also played a role. Finally, the strong tendency to concentrate material and human resources on elite education has forced many students to leave the system.

However, the statistics also show that the decline in enrolment stopped around 1983. In the senior section, total enrolment figures have actually been

---

27. *ZGJYB*, 21 May, 1987, p. 2.

going up since then, thanks to the expansion of vocational education. This tendency reflects a growing awareness of the importance of popular education after some years of exclusive concern for the elite, and this leaves room for some optimism about future development in Chinese secondary school enrolment.

7. Selection and Competition[1]

The increased importance of the selective function of secondary schools, the revised criteria and methods for selecting students for secondary and tertiary education and the subsequent competitive and elitist atmosphere in middle schools will be the starting point for a discussion of the qualitiative aspects of the post-Mao reforms in secondary education. As discussed in Chapter 4, access to education plays a crucial role in the social distribution process in China. It is therefore natural that the entire process of reform in secondary education was initiated by changes in this field, and that these changes have been more vehemently debated than any other during the reform decade.

After a brief historical introduction to the question of educational selection in China, the present chapter proceeds to discuss three major elements of the meritocratic and elitist wave in China's education system during the last decade: the reintroduction of exams and tests, the division between "key" and "non-key" schools and the streaming of students into "fast" and "slow" classes. The consequences of these three policies highlight the tremendous influence exercised by changes in selection procedure on the form and content of education and exemplify the close relationship between educational reform and a host of other social and political questions.

Exams and Selection Before 1977
The traditional Chinese way of selecting and promoting bureaucrats acquired great fame for its adherence to meritocratic principles at a time when birth and wealth were the prime criteria for achieving public posts in Europe.[2] The Chinese tradition for institutionalized meritocratic selection of officials has roots back to the times of the Han dynasty more than two thousand years ago. A civil service examination system, which, with some interruptions, remained effective until the beginning of this century was introduced in the 7th century during the Sui and Tang dynasties. Three features in particular characterized the traditional examination system in its ideal form. First of all, it was meritocratic. While

---

1. An earlier version of this chapter has been published as an article in *The Australian Journal of Chinese Affairs*, cf. *Thøgersen 1989*.

2. For the traditional examination system see *Hu 1984* and *Miyazaki 1976*.

women were excluded, men from almost all social classes could try their luck at the examinations and thus enter the class of bureaucrats. Though access to education was, of course, much easier for children of wealthy families than for others, the examination system seems to have guaranteed a certain degree of social mobility in traditional Chinese society.[3] Much was done to avoid cheating and corruption, and though these countermeasures were never fully successful, public confidence in the system seems to have been considerable, and the general prestige of the exams remained high right up to the late 19th century. Secondly, the exams tested moral superiority, as expressed in one's mastery of the Confucian classics, rather than practical knowledge or skills useful in the daily work of an official. Thirdly, passing the examinations and becoming an official was the key to a number of important social and legal benefits, not only for the candidate himself but also for his family.[4] Exams were, in short, the gateway to success in imperial China.

Access to tertiary education remained a matter of great importance not only during the Republican period, but also in the People's Republic. As mentioned in Chapter 2, different methods and criteria of selection were tried out between 1949 and 1976. Students' academic achievements, class background and political behaviour were always considered, but the relative importance of these three criteria varied widely, and each policy of selection turned out to have its own flaws.

After the fall of the "Gang of Four", admission and selection policies could not just be copied from the past. "Political behaviour" had become synonymous with "connections" in the eyes of the public and was furthermore rooted in a period during which the CCP had the moral prestige to define right and wrong in politics. This was not the case in the late 1970s, when the Party was deeply shaken by the Cultural Revolution. The "class background" criterion was becoming increasingly irrelevant, as it was based on the pre-1949 status of a person's family and thus said little about the family's present socio-economic position. Any construction of a new classification on sociological grounds would have been politically disastrous for the attempts to heal the wounds of the Cultural Revolution; it would have brought the question of the class structure of socialist China back on the agenda, and thereby particularly alienate the intellectuals, whose support was essential to the "Four Modernizations"

---

3. *Ho 1962*. For an interesting compilation of texts on the question of social mobility through the imperial examination system see also *Menzel 1963*.

4. *Ch'ü 1965*, particularly pp. 177-185.

campaign. Thus, in the minds of the new leaders only one course remained: selection had to be based almost exclusively on academic criteria.

Exams in Command

As mentioned in Chapter 2 (see Table 2.1), the transition from senior secondary to tertiary education became a bottleneck in China's educational system during the sixties and seventies, and the selection taking place at this point was beset with political and social conflicts. It was therefore natural that the reform of selection methods began with the introduction of national university entrance exams.

University entrance exams were, in fact, already held for the 1977 entrants (who in reality did not start their studies until early 1978), but only at the provincial level. In October, 1977, however, it was announced that future university students were to be selected on the basis of a unified national examination for the first time since 1965. Candidates were also to pass a physical checkup and go through a political screening, but the academic test was to be by far the most important element. This decision exercised a tremendous influence on Chinese secondary education throughout the following decade, where the university entrance exam became the guideline for almost all teaching activities. The announcement claimed that even the political level of the students would be reflected adequately in their exam score:

> To ensure enrolment quality, it is essential to adhere to the principle of making overall evaluation morally, intellectually and physically and of selecting outstanding students for enrolment. An academic achievement test is one of the important ways to examine the students' political theory and educational level, and also one of the major means to select outstanding students for enrolment.[5]

This way of linking political reliability to academic achievements was also reflected in the admissions policy of the Communist Youth League, which in many cases started to demand that only students with high marks could become members. The fact that university students in increasing numbers should be recruited directly from the most recent senior middle school graduates without demanding any practical work experience from them also strengthened the position of academic criteria.

---

5. *RMRB*, 21 October 1977, p.1. Translation from SWB/FE/5648/BII/4-6 (24 Oct 77).

After the introduction of national university entrance examinations, Chinese educational cadres and teachers at all levels of the educational system became almost obsessed with tests and exams. Soon parents were sending their children to participate in tests before their first day in primary school in order to decide whether they would go to a key or an ordinary school, and the same method of selection was used in deciding all the later stages of a child's educational career: access to the next level of schooling, selection for general or vocational education, etc.... Exams were normally held in all subjects two to three times each term, and weekly tests were common in most subjects. In 1986 it was calculated that a Chinese student from the time he or she entered primary school to the senior secondary school final examination had gone through between ninety and one hundred screenings based on academic tests.[6]

One official argument for this multitude of tests was that they served the purpose of showing teachers as well as students the strong and weak points in the teaching/learning process and thus were useful in readjusting teaching methods.[7] Exams were also seen as a disciplining and motivating force, politically as well as academically.[8] The most important argument was, however, that exams were the most just and reliable tool for selecting talented people. Only this selective function can explain the enormous investment in them of time and material resources: they determined students' further careers and were therefore loaded with social importance, not only for the students, but also for society, which needs the right person to be placed in the right job. But were the exams, then, a reliable way of selecting "talented people"? In other words, what degree of validity did Chinese exams and tests have?

The validity of tests
Chinese research on test validity has focused on the university entrance examination. Three main questions were raised in the early 1980s: 1) what was tested in this examination, 2) was the evaluation of exam papers fair, and 3) did the exam manage to select the students best suited for higher education?

---

6. *JYYJ* no. 8, 1986, pp. 18-22.

7. This is the main argument, for example, in an official textbook on education like: *Huazhong Shifan 1984*, pp. 15-20.

8. See for example *RMRB*, 21 October 1977, p. 1, where it states that "selecting those with the most outstanding level for college enrolment" was the only way to "encourage young people to follow the correct political orientation and devote themselves to study scientific and cultural knowledge."

In this period, there seemed to be a general consensus among Chinese educators that the entrance exams mainly tested students' ability in memorization. The following judgment passed in 1981 by Chen Yuanhui in *Educational Research*, for example, was rarely contradicted: "When we analyse the direction and content of the university entrance examinations in certain subjects, we find to a large degree that they solely test memory and neither thinking ability nor intelligence".[9]

That knowledge *(zhishi)* as tested in exams was something fundamentally different from the ability *(nengli)* to apply knowledge in practice and to solve problems, and that the highest scoring students were therefore not necessarily those who had the best grasp of the practical methods in a certain field has also been documented by Chinese research.[10] During the last few years several proposals have been put forth for testing ability rather than knowledge, but no fundamental change seems to have taken place so far.

The evaluation of exam papers was another dubious point. Much was done to avoid pressure on, or direct corruption of, examiners,[11] but even if such malpractices could have been stopped, large problems would still have remained. As early as in 1980, Chinese research found that the same examination paper received very different marks when evaluated by different teachers.[12] A later Chinese survey made the same point and further noted that the questions were too few and of too low a quality to reflect students' actual academic level. It concluded that: "We have not treated examinations...as a science that should be the object of research, and this has made us grope in the dark".[13]

Some of the researchers behind the latter survey dealt an even harder blow to university entrance examinations in their conclusions to a survey of the correlation between students' scores in the entrance examination and their later academic achievements at university:

There is very little correlation between university entrance examination scores and university study achievements, which demonstrates the lack of

9. *JYYJ* no. 2, 1981, p. 15-20 (p. 19).

10. *JYYJ* no. 10, 1982, pp. 34-42.

11. This work is described in detail in *Pepper 1984*.

12. *JYYJ* no. 6, 1980, pp. 45-47.

13. *JYYJ* no. 6, 1983, pp. 50-57.

predictive value of the university entrance examination. As a forecast with a selective function the present entrance examination method has failed.[14]

It is interesting to note that the same survey found a high correlation between entrance examination scores and *secondary school* achievements. Moreover, it disclosed that secondary school teachers had developed a remarkable ability to predict the fate of their students on the entrance examination. This must reflect the fact that secondary school teachers had to a large extent adapted their teaching to the demands of the examination, while the examination authorities were careful to make the exams predictable and in accordance with the secondary school curriculum, thereby guaranteeing the carrot-and-stick function of the entrance examinations for secondary school students. A survey of medical school students showed that *large* differences in entrance examination scores did correlate with the students' score in the final medical examination, but no correlation was found when students' scores were largely inside the same range.[15] The same survey showed a positive correlation between pre-university work experience inside the medical field and final medical exam score, which is interesting in view of the fact that subject-related work experience does not help young Chinese get into university. All the problems surrounding the use of tests and exams mentioned above have been found in Western countries as well, but in spite of the considerable interest in post-Mao China for Western educational theory, Chinese decision makers have not paid much attention to this type of critical research, at least not until quite recently.[16]

These first results of Chinese research into the question of test validity around 1980 were rather controversial, considering the importance of exams in Chinese education. It was shown that the university entrance examination tested memory, not intelligence or skill, that it was virtually impossible to evaluate exam papers fairly, and that exam scores did not correlate with university achievements. In short, this kind of exam was unsuited for selective purposes. Considering that the university entrance examination was much more carefully prepared and supervised than the selective tests used at the lower levels of the educational system, the value of these other tests must have been very poor indeed.

---

14. *JYYJ* no. 6, 1985, pp. 54-61.

15. *JYYJ* no. 10, 1985, pp. 51-55.

16. For a presentation of Western results strikingly similar to the Chinese ones see *Kvale 1972*.

Critique of the examination system

While the question of test validity appears to only have attracted the attention of a limited number of educational experts in the early 1980s, other effects of the examination system aroused deep public concern. Students' motivation and diligence had improved relative to the early seventies, but the price for this progress was high, particularly in primary and secondary education, where the influence of what the Chinese call "the one-sided tendency to seek higher transition rates" (*pianmian zhuiqiu shengxuelü*) was heavily felt. This phenomenon was criticized by Jiang Nanxiang, then Minister of Education, as early as 1979.[17] The term describes the tendency to see the main objective of education not as the transmission of technical and ideological qualifications that would enable students to fill their role in Chinese society, but rather as the selection of the students best suited for higher education and the preparation of these students for competitive examinations. This led to a situation where first and second year students as well as students with low test scores were ignored to the benefit of students in the final year of junior and senior middle school and students with high scores. Furthermore, it encouraged a teaching method that stressed rote learning of facts relevant for the examinations rather than the development of students' actual skills. Finally, it exposed students and teachers to an enormous psychological pressure from parents and ambitious local cadres who wanted "their" schools to be first in the competition on transition rates. In many cases teachers' bonuses became directly related to the number of students in their class who passed the entrance examination to the next level and to the average scores of his or her class on the tests. Likewise, students were rewarded by their parents if they gained admittance to a prestigeous school and often heavily punished if they did not.

The problem was and is recognized as extremely serious by educators at all levels. In 1983, for example, Vice-minister of Education Zhang Jian gave the following pessimistic picture of Chinese education after the examination reforms:

> In present day middle schools, exams inhibit teaching rather than promote it. A profusion of questions join together to form a wave in a sea of exams, tests and final examinations deluging students, teachers and even parents. In general middle schools the pursuit of higher transition rates ties the hands

---

17. *RMJY* no. 6, 1979, pp. 3-8.

and feet of teachers and students like an invisible rope. Even when we look at academic education, we have failed.[18]

Likewise, many students have complained about the pressure from the examination system. The following exerpt from a middle school student's letter to the youth magazine *China's Youth* is a typical example of the tone in these protests:

What I fear most is to fail at the university entrance examination. We are all racing down a trail as narrow as a sheep's intestines. All of us want to get to the goal, but there is always the danger of being forced out. From primary through secondary school to university we constantly squeeze our way down the narrow track, students competing, schools competing, even parents and teachers competing. We are all dancing to the pipe of the entrance exam until we lose our breath.[19]

Such criticisms, not of exams as such, but of their negative side effects have constantly been published in newspapers and educational magazines ever since 1978, and recently some revisions have been made. Before turning to the most recent discussion of selection and exams, however, it would be useful to look at two other hotly debated issues related to the question of selection: key schools and streaming.

Key Schools

Key schools (*zhongdian xuexiao*) are elite institutions which enjoy a number of privileges in regard to recruitment of students and teachers and to financial support.[20] Already in May, 1977, only eight months after the fall of the Cultural Revolution leaders, Deng Xiaoping proclaimed that China would reintroduce the key school system from primary through secondary to tertiary education,[21] and in January, 1978 an official decision on the question was published.[22] This was an unmistakable signal that more attention should be paid to the education of the elite. Up to 1966, key schools had existed all over the country, but during the

---

18. *JYYJ* no. 6, 1983, pp. 11-15.

19. *ZGQN* no. 20, 1981, p. 2.

20. The most exhaustive discussion of the implementation of the key school policy is in *Rosen 1987*. See also *Rosen 1984* and *Pepper 1984*, particularly pp. 20-30. An English translation of important Chinese articles on key schools can be found in: *CE*, vol. 17, no. 2, Summer 1984.

21. *Deng 1984*, pp. 53-54.

22. *RMRB*, 25 January, 1978, p. 1.

Cultural Revolution they were closed down as symbols of educational elitism, accused of bringing up future aristocrats isolated from the people. By rehabilitating the key school system without even changing the name, Deng showed his loyalty to the pre-Cultural Revolution heritage and his conviction that the training of top-level scientists ought to have higher priority than the pursuit of egalitarian political goals.

Not unexpectedly, the key school strategy immediately met widespread opposition among cadres in the educational field. In late 1978 a number of articles appeared in different corners of China complaining that local cadres were resisting the implementation of the new policy.[23] Some officials openly accused the key school strategy of "concentrating on the minority while losing the majority",[24] and they seemed to have support from many teachers and parents. As a clear hint that opposition to the key school policy would be treated as hidden support for the educational policies of the "Gang of Four", the new leadership accused educational cadres of having worked with more enthusiasm during the Cultural Revolution, when they were said to have carried out reforms in spite of resistance from parents, teachers and students.[25] Many non-key schools also joined the opposition, for example by discouraging their best students from applying for a place in a key school. Their purpose was, of course, to keep for themselves as many talented students as possible in order to improve their own transition rates, and perhaps thus advance to key school status themselves.[26]

This competition among schools was reduced when a National Key School Work Conference was held in July, 1980. By this time Hua Guofeng, though still formally Party chairman, and other leaders associated with Mao Zedong and the Cultural Revolution had lost power, while the reform wing led by Deng Xiaoping had gained control over the Party and state apparatus. This paved the way for a stabilization of the key school strategy. The conference recommended a further concentration of resources on a reduced number of schools, only 700 at the secondary school level. The key status of these schools would, however, be of a more permanent nature to avoid constant competition among schools. The conference also warned local authorities against putting too much emphasis on

---

23. Three such reports from Hunan, Guangdong and Xinjiang from December 1978 were reprinted ZXXJY no. 12, 1978, pp. 58-62.

24. Ibid., p. 58.

25. Ibid., p. 59.

26. Beijing Ribao (Beijing Daily) 17 June, 1979.

transition rates when evaluating the quality of a school.[27] This could be seen as a concession, at least at the verbal level, to the critics of elitist excesses.

The ambiguous role of key schools

The decisions of the Work Conference did not, however, stop criticisms of the key school policy, and it became more and more evident that even supporters of the policy were not in full agreement about the role of the key schools inside the educational system. Some saw them primarily as hothouses for the future elite, while others stressed their function as models for other schools. This ambiguity led to continued conflicts surrounding the key school issue.

When Deng Xiaoping first mentioned the idea of reintroducing the key school system, it was in connection with the need to train a small contingent of highly qualified scientists.[28] Though not directly stated, his idea was obviously that key schools should cultivate future university students and thereby constitute an elite track all way up through the educational system. This goal has to a large degree been achieved, as can be seen from the fact that many of the best key middle schools developed close ties with tertiary level institutions. This tie, called "*guagou*", means that the students of the secondary school can use the facilities of the university, that university teachers come to the secondary school to give lectures and that the graduates of the secondary school enjoy certain privileges when applying for entrance to the university. It is thus taken for granted that the key middle school students of today will be the university students of tomorrow. In 1984, 80% of the Shanghai senior middle school graduates recruited by tertiary level schools came from the city's sixteen key middle schools, while less than 20% were recruited from the more than 270 non-key schools.[29] In Beijing and other large cities the top key schools have transition rates very close to 100%, and the large majority of their students are recruited by key universities.[30]

The "hothouse" conception of the key school strategy has been dominant in most places throughout the last ten years, not only in the cities, where students have a realistic hope of getting access to university, but also in rural districts

---

27. *RMJY* no. 9, 1980, p. 3-9. A list of the 695 top priority key schools is found in *Zhongguo Jiaoyu Nianjian 1949-1981*, p. 1096-1103.

28. *Deng 1984*, pp. 53-54.

29. *ZXXJY* no. 4, 1986, pp. 15-20. For more evidence see *Rosen 1984*, pp. 84-85, and *Pepper 1984*, pp. 24-26.

30. This was the case, for example, at Beijing Normal University's No. 2 Attached Middle School, which I visited in 1984.

where funds are scarce and an even higher degree of concentration is therefore necessary in order to keep up with the city schools. In Haicheng County, Liaoning, for instance, it was already decided as early as in 1977 to concentrate resources on only one key middle school. This school later achieved the status of a provincial level key school. Forty-two teachers with university background and considerable teaching experience were transferred to the school from other middle schools in the county. The county further provided furniture and building materials for the reconstruction of the school and in two years gave it 264,000 *yuan* in extra funds. During the same period the county Party secretary paid visits to the school on no less than seven occasions.[31] Such a concentration of money and personnel seems to have been the rule rather than the exception in rural areas and could, of course, only be achieved at the expense of other schools in the same county.

But in official statements key schools are not described as elite institutions as such. Quite to the contrary, it is often stressed that they have the same "double responsibility" as other schools in training future workers for the productive sectors as well as in cultivating future university students. The key schools, according to this definition, should function as models for non-key schools, and the only difference should be the generally higher quality of their work.[32] After the reduction and stabilization of the number of key schools in 1980, their position became more secure and there was more room for experimenting with new teaching methods and spreading these "advanced experiences" to other schools. Only in a few places, however, did cooperation between key and non-key schools seem to have become systematic and close. One obvious reason for this is that the quality of human and material resources of the two kinds of schools was so different that the experiences of the key school teachers were difficult to transfer to their less favoured colleagues.

That key schools have generally failed to fulfill their function as models does not mean that the elitist line was ever exclusively implemented. If key schools were to constitute a genuine elite track preparing future university students, leaving it to the non-key schools to train manpower for the lower levels of the job hierarchy, it would have been necessary to break with the pre-1966 model and develop separate curricula, separate teaching materials and even separate teaching methods for each of the two tracks, thus explicitly preparing the

---

31. *Jiaoyubu 1980*, pp. 244-249.

32. For an authoritative definition of the role of key schools see *Zhongguo Jiaoyu Nianjian 1949-1981*, pp. 167-170.

students for different career patterns. For ideological reasons, however, it was never possible to go so far with the key school strategy: the Maoist legacy proved too strong to allow such blatantly elitist measures. It is my personal impression that the key schools do to some degree bring up people with leadership qualities. In my questionnaire survey in Yantai (cf. Chapter 10), the key school students gave much more independent answers than other students to questions on how they liked going to school and what they would like to change in their education. Likewise, in a senior secondary key school class in Beijing, where I sat in for a week in 1984, I found the students very conscious of their own future leadership role in China.[33] Officially, however, key schools to a great extent have had to stick to the same teaching plans and teaching methods as the non-key schools in spite of the fact that they have had better teachers, better students, better equipment and more money than other schools.

Two opposing forces in Chinese society seem to have fought a battle over the key schools, a battle which both of them have lost. Deng Xiaoping and the reform wing were never allowed a free hand to fully develop an elite track for preparing a relatively small number of students for academic careers. Pressure from local cadres, teachers and parents forced them to moderate this strategy. The more egalitarian educators were able to defend the principle, also recognized before the Cultural Revolution, that key and non-key schools should fulfil the same functions, but they were forced to accept the fact that a redistribution favouring the elite took place inside the educational system via the key schools, and that access to university education was normally gained through a key school career. The unfortunate consequence of this compromise was that education in non-key general schools became primarily aimed at preparing students for a higher education to which they had only minimal chances of ever getting access.

Key schools on the defensive
Constant complaints that the concentration of resources in key schools led to the neglect of the large majority of the students have from the early 1980s forced the key school supporters on the defensive. In the first half of 1982, for instance, leading cadres in many provinces had to stand up and defend the key schools against massive public opposition,[34] and in 1985 it was reported that some cities

---

33. This school was Beijing Normal University's No. 2 Attached Middle School.

34. See, for example *Sichuan Jiaoyu* (*Sichuan Education*) no. 2, 1982, pp. 3ff., *Beijing Jiaoyu* (*Beijing Education*) no. 2, 1982, pp. 3-6, *Nei Menggu Jiaoyu* (*Inner Mongolian Education*) no. 5-6, 1982, pp. 19-23.

had already abolished the key school system.[35] Since then little positive news has been heard about the key school system in the media. Some localities have, on the contrary, reported that the abolition of key schools at the primary and junior secondary level has been a great success,[36] and in many places students at these two levels are now recruited according to geographic rather than academic criteria. At the senior secondary level, however, the position of the key schools remains unweakened.

Even where the key school system has officially been abolished, changes should not be overestimated. There has been nothing to indicate that the teachers and equipment of the former key schools are now being distributed to other schools. The politically most important change is in the field of student recruitment, where the neighborhood principle is now more widely used. This could be expected to change the present situation, where children of intellectuals and cadres are overrepresented in key schools (cf. Chapter 10). However, although the neighborhood principle may moderate this tendency, it should be kept in mind that many key schools are run by universities or placed in other areas with a high concentration of intellectual and cadre families. Though the key school debate was rather quiet in the late 1980s, the basic dilemma is still unresolved at the theoretical as well as at the practical level: should China's educational system continue to have a separate elite track, and how much funding should be allocated to this system in relation to ordinary schools?

Streaming
University entrance examinations and key schools became the prime symbols of the post-1977 meritocratic trend in Chinese education and have been the most important reforms in this direction at the structural level. But psychologically, the division of students inside each school into different streams based on academic aptitude was probably just as important. A variety of designations have been used for these streams, but the most common ones, which shall also be used here, are "fast" and "slow" classes (*kuai ban / man ban*), in some cases with a "medium" class (*zhong ban*) in between.

The origin of the streaming system differs from that of the key school strategy in that no central document seems to have initiated the use of this method, and no authoritative figure has backed it from the outset. Nor did it have a pre-Cultural Revolution tradition to use as a reference. On the contrary, it

---

35. *BR* no. 18, 1985, pp. 9-10.

36. *ZXXJY* no. 3, 1987, pp. 15-16.

seems to have originated as a local response to problems facing secondary education after the introduction of the national college entrance examinations in 1977. As higher transition rates became linked with the allocation of more resources, each school wanted to qualify at least some of its students for the next level of schooling and therefore gathered its most promising into special classes. Streaming in Gansu Province, for instance, was sparked off by newspaper articles:

> In February last year (1978) when the *People's Daily* had presented the experiences of some Beijing middle schools in structuring classes on the basis of students' academic performance, all schools under the Lanzhou Education Bureau split up their classes and reconstructed them according to students' actual academic level.[37]

There were two main arguments for streaming middle school students. One was that the variation in academic level between students of the same age, because of the disruptive influence on education of the "Gang of Four", was so large that both "fast" and "slow" students would benefit from the division. The other argument was parallel to the justifications of the key school system: the country needed a "fast training of qualified personnel" (*kuai chu rencai*), and this training would be more efficient if the brightest students were brought together.

Resistance to streaming was widespread from the beginning, and since, unlike the key school strategy, it was not official national policy, this resistance was allowed to express itself rather freely in the media. In Shanxi, for example, the February, 1978 issue of the provincial education magazine, which invited readers to take part in a discussion on how to train qualified personnel as fast as possible, carried an article recommending streaming.[38] But in the April issue, the Party branch of a village middle school opposed this view. The article carried the title "We shall certainly not let a single class brother or sister fall behind", thereby indicating the political implications of the question, and argued that mutual cooperation and learning from each other inside the classroom was preferable to competitive streaming.[39] The dispute was never settled but bounced back and forth in the media for years. Some tried to make compromises, theoretical as well as practical, between the elitist and the egalitarian trends, but the

---

37. *Gansu Ribao* (*Gansu Daily*), 22 February, 1979, p. 3.

38. *Shanxi Jiaoyu* no. 2, 1978, pp. 16-17.

39. *Shanxi Jiaoyu* no. 4, 1978, pp. 22-23.

chasm between Maoist egalitarianism and Dengist elitism was too deep in the late 1970s. Two debaters, representing respectively the elitist and the egalitarian viewpoints, had articles published in *Educational Research* in 1979, the content of which clearly illustrate the large divergence of opinions.

Sun Zhen, who represented the elitist view, primarily concerned himself with the question of how to bring up "a sufficient number of high level scientists, engineers and experts in all fields".[40] Based on Western as well as Chinese experience he argued that 1) children should start their education earlier, preferably in kindergarten, in order to let the most talented of them graduate from university at a younger age; 2) key schools and streaming were suitable methods of securing a high standard in the education of future scientists; and 3) more money should be invested in higher education. Though the three points are interrelated, I shall concentrate here on the second one.

Sun finds that one reason for the lack of qualified people in China is the prevailing egalitarian ideology not only during but also before and after the Cultural Revolution decade. China must start to "teach students according to their abilities" (*yin cai shi jiao*) and recognize the importance of the free development of individuals. The "top students" (*jianzi*) must be picked out as early as possible and trained in special classes in order to meet the demands of the social division of labour. He therefore finds it deplorable that "there is resistance against key schools in some provinces and cities" and that streaming "has been met almost with reproach". As long as the less talented students get a decent education and are not neglected by the schools, streaming is "totally in accordance with the basic interests of the proletariat and the needs of the four modernizations".

Sun Zhen is in many ways a typical representative of the advocates of streaming and early selection in the late 1970s. First of all he considers only one function of education, i.e. the transmission of technical qualifications, and he relates these qualifications exclusively to the production process and not to students' future roles as citizens in Chinese society. He takes the existing division of labour for granted and has no ambitions of changing it through the education system. He concerns himself with neither the moral and political content of education nor its sociological and psychological effects. His emphasis on technical qualifications leads him to regard students as mere vessels into which as much knowledge as possible should be poured as quickly as possible.

---

40. Sun Zhen: "Duo chu rencai, kuai chu rencai, zao chu rencai qianyi" ("My simple opinion on the extensive, fast and early training of talented personel") *JYYJ* no. 5, 1979, pp. 16-22.

Though Sun Zhen's views certainly represent the dominant line of thought in the late seventies and early eighties, voices of opposition were also heard. In the same issue of *Educational Research*, for instance, Ma Jixiong argues that China's education system should be "egalitarian" (*pingdeng zhuyi*) rather than "elitist" (*jianzi zhuyi*).[41] He stresses the fact that students will grow up to be citizens and not just members of the work force, and that it is therefore necessary to provide them with a common bulk of basic knowledge. Furthermore, he states that no reliable methods have yet been developed to select the students best suited for academic careers, which means that the whole streaming process is largely an arbitrary one. On these grounds he opposes not only streaming inside general schools, but also the vocationalization of part of the middle schools.

It is characteristic that Ma quotes Hua Guofeng's slogan on "elevating the scientific and cultural level of the entire Chinese people" rather than Deng Xiaoping's demand to "bring talented people up fast", as the general mood of his article is far from the competitive and elitist spirit of the Dengists. Unlike Sun Zhen, Ma sees basic general education of all future citizens as a justified political demand of the people, thereby recognizing the often ignored point that education influences students' qualifications for taking part in political and social life as well as in production. He does suggest that the abilities and interests of individual students should be given consideration, but when it comes to how this can be done in a classroom with 60 students, his only suggestion is to allow some students to graduate in advance of their classmates. The failure of the egalitarians to show how the quality of education can be raised for all students, while simultaneously encouraging individual development without the use of streaming is an obvious weak point in their argumentation.

Negative effects of streaming

While this theoretical discussion was going on, with both sides making a broad use of foreign experiences as arguments, realities in Chinese schools soon made all of the involved parties realize some of the dangers of the elitist strategy.

The most important problem discussed at this time was that conditions in the "medium" and "slow" classes in many schools had become intolerable. A report from Gansu describes the atmosphere of a "slow" class in a senior middle school:

---

41. Ma Jixiong: "Cong tigao zhengge Zhonghua minzu de kexue wenhua shuiping kan woguo de zhongdeng jiaoyu jiegou" ("The structure of Chinese secondary education seen in the light of raising the scientific and cultural level of the entire Chinese people") *JYYJ* no. 5, 1979, pp. 41-44.

It was a chemistry lesson. A young female teacher was lecturing on ... a junior middle school topic. Not all students were present. Out of 47 students only 32 attended this lesson. The classroom was filthy... The unoccupied seats were covered with a thick layer of dust... Two students were fighting for fun, several were talking across the tables, one was openly humming a tune and one hit the student in front of him with his fist... The teacher talked on as if she was used to this state of affairs in the classroom, and she was obviously powerless.[42]

Several other negative effects of streaming were mentioned in the press. Sometimes, more than 80 students were put into one "slow" class to secure better conditions for the "fast" students.[43] The "slow" classes were assigned inexperienced and incompetent teachers, the students often felt ashamed and rejected, and they quickly lost their enthusiasm for studying. The fact that "naughty" students were often placed in slow classes regardless of their academic level contributed to the disciplinary problems in these classes. The psychological consequences of streaming were probably more serious than those of the key/non-key division, because "slow" students attended the same schools as "fast" students and were in this way reminded daily of their inadequacy.

The negative effects of this heavy-handed screening soon became evident to most people in the educational field, and some debaters even started blaming the high dropout rates on the practice of streaming.[44] In September 1979, Shanghai decided to stop streaming and only maintain a few classes for students with special problems.[45] But the central authorities did not intervene to stop streaming on a national scale. On the contrary, Minister of Education Jiang Nanxiang stated in July, 1979 that streaming was still necessary. Though Jiang stressed that education should benefit all students, not just the "fast" ones,[46] these moral/political arguments had limited effect on the extremely competitive atmosphere existing in Chinese schools.

Opposition to streaming continued all through 1980. Some provinces, like Shanxi, which had remained very sceptical to streaming throughout the reform

---

42. *Gansu Ribao*, 14 January, 1979, p. 1.

43. *Jilin Ribao (Jilin Daily)*, 13 March, 1979, p. 3.

44. *Jilin Ribao*, 30 March, 1979, p. 3.

45. *GMRB*, 6 September, 1979, p. 1.

46. *GMRB*, 18 July, 1979, p. 1.

process, stopped streaming in elementary schools and key middle schools, but let other middle schools decide for themselves whether they would split up the students or not.[47] In 1981, the focus of criticism shifted from the poor conditions in the "slow" classes to the miserable life of the "fast" students. For some time, warnings had been issued against damaging the health of these students by putting them under too heavy pressure from homework, exams and tests,[48] and this had led some provinces like Shanxi, Shandong, Shaanxi and Liaoning to completely stop the practice of streaming from the beginning of the autumn term.[49] Finally, in January 1982, the Ministry of Education recommended in very vague terms that streaming should be reduced and that classes should at least cease to be *called* "fast" and "slow".[50]

Although the central authorities have generally discouraged streaming since 1982, exceptions can easily be found. In late 1983, for instance, *Chinese Education News* carried a couple of articles describing the positive results of streaming in Chongqing, Sichuan Province, where streaming had officially been stopped in 1981, and in Hangzhou, where about 40% of all senior middle school students were placed in special classes (*not* called "slow", however) which followed a reduced curriculum. An editorial comment praised this policy.[51]

Other articles, though opposed to streaming, confirm that it is still a widespread practice. In 1986, middle schools in Dalian were reported to be divided into three groups according to the academic level of their students, and inside each school students were again split up into classes of different academic levels.[52] In Xuzhou, 70% of all junior middle schools still streamed their students in 1984, and though streaming was less common at this level in 1986, it was still almost universal in the city's senior middle schools.[53] In 1987 complaints about streaming were still seen in the press.[54] That streaming still is an important factor in the life of many Chinese students despite protests from students, parents and

---

47. *Shanxi Jiaoyu* no. 1, 1980, pp. 4-5.

48. See, for example, *JYYJ* no. 1, 1981, pp. 28, 37-39.

49. *Jiaoyu Dashiji*, entry 81111, p. 627.

50. *Jiaoyu Dashiji*, entry 8213, p. 645.

51. *ZGJYB*, 24 November, 1983, p. 1.

52. *Dalian Ribao (Dalian Daily)*, 4 April, 1986, p. 3.

53. *Jiaoyu lilun yu shijian (Educational Theory and Practice)* (Taiyuan) no. 3, 1986, p. 49. From *ZXXJY* no. 7, 1986, p. 13.

54. *ZGJYB*, 12 March, 1987, p. 2.

teachers and despite official disapproval serves to illustrate the force of the examination system.

Moderation of the Examination System

The first wave of reform of secondary education after 1977 was meritocratic in the sense that academic qualifications became the prime criterion for selection, and elitist in the sense that resources were concentrated around the cultivation of "talents" for the top of the job hierarchy. The reforms had, as we have seen, serious negative side effects for the entire educational system. The central educational bureaucracy reacted to these new problems first with moral lectures and later, when this proved to have little effect, with a moderation of the key school policy and official discouragement of streaming, they being the most conspicuous examples of early division and selection of children. The sharply reduced student intake in general senior middle school was also expected to make competition for entrance to university less rigorous.

It soon became evident, however, that these measures alone did not solve the problem. Access to university was still very restricted, and as selection was still based on exams, exams continued to constitute the vital stepping stones in a person's educational career and to dictate the form and content of education. In mid-1986 the pictures drawn of school life in the Chinese media were as gloomy as ever,[55] the examination system was criticized sharply and reforms were even suggested by cadres of the Education Commission.[56] The student demonstrations in the winter of 1986-87 increased many leaders' doubts about the value of the university entrance examinations and the use of academic selection criteria in general. If students selected through exams turned against the Party, did that not show, in the eyes of the Party, that the examination system had failed to select the right people?[57]

This, together with the other negative effects of elitism and competition mentioned above, has led to a number of reforms during the last few years. Much work has been carried out to develop ways of evaluating schools and teachers without only looking at transition rates. In areas where junior secondary

---

55. For examples, see *JYYJ* no. 4, 1986, pp. 6-12 and no. 5, pp. 11-13.

56. Yang Xuewei: "Pianmian zhuiqiu shengxuelü yu kaoshi jingzheng" ("The One-sided Tendency to Seek Higher Transition Rates and Exam Competition"), *JYYJ* no. 1, 1987, 45-49.

57. For a typical lamentation of how today's students lack the moral qualities of former times see the editorial of *RMRB*, 28 April, 1987, p. 1.

school has been made universal, entrance exams to this level are being abolished, and the number of tests is to be reduced in all secondary schools.[58]

In addition, university admission procedures have been changed, though not in any fundamental way. One direction of reform is towards more objective types of exams like standardized examinations and multiple-choice tests, which leave less room for subjectivity in evaluation. There are also deviations from strictly meritocratic rules. First of all, universities now have the authority to select the students they want from among those who pass the physical and political screenings and whose entrance examination scores fall inside the same twenty point range.[59] This is intended to allow universities more room for basing selection on students' political attitude and moral qualities.

Secondly, students with an examination score of up to 30 points lower than the lowest scoring ordinary students are being accepted in increasing numbers on a self-paying basis. According to one official source, the number of such students increased from "several hundred in 1985 to more than 30,000 in 1988".[60] Another source says that the real figure (because of underreporting) may be as high as 100,000,[61] a substantial figure compared to the 640,000 students enrolled through the normal procedures. There is no information on the social background of this group of students, but it seems reasonable to believe that some of them come from the new "entrepreneur" families with money (the fee is normally from 1,000 to 2,000 *yuan* a year) but without academic traditions, while others are probably paid for by overseas relatives. Other students who can now enter university with lower marks than required from others are "three good" students,[62] excellent student cadres and students who have shown special moral-political excellence or who are particularly good at sports.[63] These new criteria will make it easier for middle schools to reward political activism, thereby strengthening their ideological grip on the students.

---

58. SWB/FE/0163 B2/4 (28 May 1988).

59. Yang Xuewei: "Tan gaoxiao zhaosheng luqu tizhi de gaige" ("On the Reform of the Admission System to Higher Education"), *ZGJYB*, 13 August, 1987, p. 3.

60. SWB/FE/0397 B2/3 (1 Mar 1989).

61. *Xinhua Wenzhai (New China Digest)* no. 9, 1989, pp. 158-59, reprinted from *Daxuesheng (University Student)* no. 7, 1989.

62. In order to become a "three-good"-student (*san hao xuesheng*) a student must perform well morally/politically, academically and physically.

63. See "Putong gaodeng xuexiao zhaosheng zanxing tiaoli" ("Provisional Regulations for Admission to General Higher Level Schools"), *ZGJYB*, 30 April, 1987, p. 2. §35 and §36.

"Directional enrolment" (*dingxiang zhaosheng*) has been practised for some time and is also mentioned in the new university admission regulations.[64] According to these rules, students who bind themselves to return to their home county after graduation can be admitted with an exam score twenty points below the ordinary standard. This type of enrolment is used specifically to guarantee a certain number of teachers, agronomists and graduates in other low-prestige vocations for poor, rural areas.

"Enrolment by commission" (*weituo daipei*), where an employer (e.g. an enterprise) selects students for university and pays their training expenses, is also possible according to the new rules.[65] This could be a gateway to university for children of local elites, though it is stressed in the regulations that these students, who are accepted outside the state enrolment plan, shall normally be up to the standards of ordinary students. In 1987, 41,000 students were enrolled in this way.[66]

These deviations from strictly meritocratic principles can be seen as concessions to sectors and social groups that have had reasons for dissatisfaction with the enrolment system, primarily the parts of the elite whose children have found it difficult to gain admission to university through the examination system (entrepreneurs and cadres without academic background) and, to a lesser degree, students from poor rural areas. But they also point towards more political control over the students by re-emphasizing the ideological selection criteria. By opening alternative channels into university the new admission policies may help reduce the totally dominating influence of exams on secondary education which has been so heavily felt since 1978. But they also create room for nepotism and "back-doorism".

New ways of conducting examinations have also been tried out, particularly at the university entrance examination level. Shanghai and Zhejiang have been the test sites of a new type of exam system, where students first take a provincial level senior secondary school leaving examination (*huikao*), which shall guarantee that they are up to required standards. Those who pass and want to continue their studies in a university can then sit for an entrance examination in Chinese, Math and one or two more subjects related to the speciality they want to study (as opposed to the seven subjects previously tested at the entrance examination). At the final step of the enrolment procedure the results of both exams as well as a

---

64. Ibid., §28 and §42.

65. Ibid., §43.

66. *Zhongguo Baike Nianjian 1988*, p. 479.

number of more subjective factors are considered. The effects of this new entrance procedure are reported to be positive, and it is planned to be in use in all localities from 1994.[67] Together with the use of standardized examinations this is expected to bring about a situation where "there is little need for the students to mechanically memorize text-books and guess the answers to the questions".[68] Such optimistic reports have, however, often been heard during the last ten years only to give way to new complaints a few months later.

The examination system has thus been under heavy fire lately, and many reforms have been suggested or even carried out. However, no real alternative presents itself, and every step away from a mechanistic enrolment procedure based on examination scores will also open the door to nepotism and the influence of connection networks. Researchers from the State Education Commission have already admitted that the system of self-paying students and enrolment by commission have provided "those with money, power and connections" with a loophole to get into university.[69]

Some participants in the debate have begun to analyze the social roots of the present problems of selection. One writer, for example, declares that the privileges of the cadre stratum are the basic problem. Cadres have nice cars and good housing, they can guarantee their offspring an advantageous start in life, and the gap between them and the rest of the population is widening. As a university education is now the easiest way to become a cadre, people are willing to do practically anything to get enrolled. The origin of the "one-sided pursuit of higher transition rates" must, according to this writer, be found in this basic socio-political problem.[70] Though such frankness is unusual, similar explanations and analyses of the close tie between education and society can be found in the writings of such high ranking cadres as the director of the test center under the State Education Commission, Yang Xuewei.[71]

In reaction to the Cultural Revolution tendency to interpret educational questions in terms of class struggle, a strong desire to see education as an autonomous sector with its own objective laws was felt after 1977. A new awareness, however, of the complicated relationship between education, society and

---

67. *GMRB*, 14 June, 1987, p. 1, and *RMJY* no. 10, 1989, pp. 19-20.

68. SWB/FE/0321 B2/1 (29 Nov 88).

69. *JYYJ* no. 8, 1989, pp. 71-73.

70. Yi Ming: "Pianmian zhuiqiu shengxuelü de shehui genyuan" ("The Social Origin of the One-sided Tendency to Seek Higher Transition Rates"), *JYYJ* no. 2, 1987, pp. 48-49.

71. *JYYJ* no. 1, 1987, pp. 45-49.

politics seems to have been growing in China in the late eighties, as educators have found that some problems facing the post-Mao educational reforms cannot be solved with educational measures alone.

Conclusion

The new selection criteria and methods introduced after 1977 transformed China's educational system, in particular secondary education, almost overnight into a meritocratic, competitive and elite-oriented structure. One explanation for the educational system's relative malleability is no doubt the impact of the old Chinese tradition for selection through competitive exams, which was sketched out in the beginning of this chapter.

The examination system solved, at least partly, some of the problems inherent in the educational structure inherited from the Cultural Revolution, notably the widespread opportunities for corruption and nepotism linked with the more "political" admission criteria, and the low motivation for study among middle school students due to the lack of connection between academic achievements and later careers.

New problems soon emerged, however, no less serious than the old ones. Education became elitist and students with poor or average results were widely neglected. Teaching often degenerated into spoon-feeding students with facts and details to be memorized, leaving no room for the development of practical skills or the ability to solve problems. This led to popular dissatisfaction among teachers, students and parents, but all cures for the new illness failed, mainly because access to university was so important to all of the involved parties that noone could afford to ignore the pressure from the examination system.

One striking feature of the new selection criteria is how well they fit into the general pattern of reform ideology in post-Mao China. The central principle underlying the examination system that success and failure should be determined by one's own abilities and judged according to objective criteria is identical with the basic idea behind the market-oriented reforms of the economy. Likewise, the idea of placing the most gifted students in privileged schools and classrooms is parallel to the "let some get rich first" ideology. Both accept the use of inequality as a motivating factor. Considering that university entrance exams and key schools were already introduced in 1977 at a time when reform plans for other sectors had not yet been formulated, it seems that education has kept its role as a showcase for general ideological and political principles also after the death of Mao, and that these educational reforms can retrospectively be seen as some of the first indications of the political visions of Deng Xiaoping and the reform wing.

The need for using a reform of educational policies as a quick political signal to the public may help to explain the lack of preparation on the part of the authorities. Though the Ministry of Education must have been aware that the changes in enrolment policy would raise a host of problems, they had no time to prepare effective countermeasures. As the shock wave from the university entrance examinations moved down through the educational system local authorities plunged into all sorts of elitist excesses, many of them detrimental to overall educational goals. All other elements of the post-Mao reforms of secondary education were in some way influenced by the examination system, including the most important one: the vocationalization of secondary education, which is the subject of the next chapter.

8. Education and Production

One of the most important elements of the post-1977 reforms of secondary education, and definitely the most widely publicized, has been the vocationalization of senior middle school.[1] During the Cultural Revolution decade, Chinese secondary education was basically a one-track, general school system. Manual labour was integrated into the curriculum, and it was considered part of the education of all students irrespective of their future job, rather than a preparation for a specific vocation. During this period China won international fame for her radical attempts to break the traditional Chinese barrier between education and the world of production. With slogans such as "combine theory with practice", "combine education with labour" and "become both red and expert", China served as an example to other developing countries as well as to radical educational reformers in the West. It may therefore seem surprising that the post-Mao leadership has insisted that the young people who graduated from secondary school during the Cultural Revolution decade lacked all practical skills and had to start from scratch when they entered their work places, and that secondary education therefore had to be vocationalized in order to meet the demands of society.

One obvious explanation is, of course, that many things were not what they seemed to be during the Cultural Revolution, and that many of the lofty principles which sounded so good in the ears of radical educators abroad were not implemented. Another reason is, however, that the view of the relationship between education and production and between the school system and the surrounding society has changed.

This chapter will first discuss some theoretical aspects of the relationship between education and production, including Mao Zedong's view on this question. This is followed by a presentation of the post-1978 vocationalization process and of the different types of secondary technical and vocational schools which grew out of the reforms. Finally, after a discussion of the fate of the education-with-production principle in general secondary education, the social and political aspects of the vocationalization reform will be discussed.

---

1. The most comprehensive discussions of vocational education in China are *Risler 1989*, *Münch and Risler 1987* and *World Bank 1987*.

Theoretical Aspects of the Relationship Between Education and Production

The idea of combining education with production and theory with practice has been supported by a number of different arguments in China.

Mao Zedong's ideas on education and production, which strongly influenced Chinese educational policies up to his death, were, of course, rooted in Marxist thinking, but they were also a reaction to the dogmas of traditional Chinese education and a reflection of Mao's sceptical attitude towards intellectuals. As mentioned in Chapter 2, traditional Chinese education was moral-oriented with little emphasis on the training of practical skills, and one of the privileges of those who passed the imperial examinations was that they then could avoid manual labour, which they generally looked upon with contempt. Mao saw the intellectuals, not only those educated before 1949 but also the new breed, as potential inheritors of this attitude, and he fought many battles first with his own intellectual background and later with China's intellectual establishment over this issue.[2] Consequently Mao saw participation in production as a crucial part of the moral-political education of all students essential for overcoming the development of a feeling of superiority among the best educated.[3]

Productive work was, however, also seen as an epistemological necessity. According to Mao, "man's knowledge depends mainly on his activity in material production".[4] He later elaborated on this point and said that "...correct ideas...come from social practice and from it alone; they come from three kinds of social practice, the struggle for production, the class struggle and scientific experiment".[5] To Mao, participation in production and other practical activities were thus important elements in the learning process.

Furthermore, the poverty of particularly the rural areas of China made student participation in production a simple economic necessity, if the CCP wanted to spread education to the countryside. This was one of the experiences gained in the pre-1949 "base areas".

On top of these reasons for letting all students, no matter what job they were to perform later, do some practical work, came society's demand that the educational system carry out vocational training with the purpose of directly

---

2. See *Grieder 1981* and *Goldman 1981*.

3. Mao's view on this question is discussed in *Price 1977*, pp. 191-195 and in *Hawkins 1974*.

4. From: "On Practice". *Mao 1967*, pp. 295-309 (p. 295).

5. From: "Where Do Correct Ideas Come From". *Mao 1971*, pp. 502-504.

preparing students for different occupations. This also called for a combination of theoretical education and productive work, but of a more differentiated nature, where students acquired different specific skills, and where practical work and training were given a more important role for future workers than for those who were to continue on to tertiary education.[6]

Because the CCP had so many different reasons to support the combining of education and production, this concept has been used as a standard explanation for the implementation of several widely different policies.

First of all, labour and productive work have been seen as a natural part of *moral/political education*. When students during the Cultural Revolution were sent to work in people's communes and factories, they were supposed to learn to be loyal to the Party, to love manual labour and to identify themselves with the workers and peasants, so that they would not feel superior to these classes at a later stage of their, maybe more privileged, careers. Participation in production was thus to eliminate the "three great differences" between industry and agriculture, town and country and mental and manual labour. The aim was not, however, to provide the students with specific skills. To sweep schoolyards, spread manure or do simple assembly work in a factory may have taught middle school students what it is like to be a peasant or a worker, but it did not qualify them for skilled jobs.

Secondly, the education-with-production concept was used in connection with activities aimed at *raising funds for education* in areas and for certain types of schools where the state would or could not cover the costs. A typical example of this are the half-work-half-study-schools, where students are engaged part of the day or the year in manual labour, particularly in agricultural work. Such schools make it possible to extend education to parts of the population which cannot afford full time schooling, but they do not *integrate* education and labour, as the work done by the students is rarely related to the curriculum.

Productive and other socially useful work has furthermore been used as an opportunity for the students to *apply and test the theoretical knowledge* learned in the classroom. During the early 1970s in particular, the media often brought stories about rural middle school students testing their textbook knowledge of agriculture in experimental fields, seeing the basic principles of physics at work in machines used in factory work shops, or practicing character writing by writing letters for old peasants, etc.... A lot of this may well have been empty

---

6. An interesting discussion on the conflicts between different aspects of the relationship between education, work and practice can be found in *Löfstedt 1987*.

propaganda, as it is now claimed, but the idea, at least, of strengthening students' learning processes and motivation through participation in practical work was very much alive at that time.[7]

Finally, during the 1950s, when China was under Soviet influence, a system of workers' training schools and secondary specialized schools was established to *train middle level technicians and skilled workers*. Practical training and productive work was an integrated part of the curriculum of such schools.

The economic, moral/political, pedagogical and job-preparatory purposes of combining education with production and theory with practice, are, however, often mutually contradictory, for example when the kind of work most profitable for the school does not match the students' intellectual level or the curriculum, when students for political reasons are told to do simple manual labour which takes time away from their other study activities, or when the streaming of students in vocational and general schools divides future workers from future intellectuals, thus counteracting the egalitarian aim of other education-with-production activities.

The complexity of the concept of education-with-production serves to explain how both the Cultural Revolution leaders and their opponents, the post-Mao reformers, could pay tribute to it while carrying out totally different policies. Before 1978, education was combined with production mainly for economic and moral-political reasons. After 1978 the stress has been on vocational training. During both periods the pedagogical argument, which calls for adapting productive activities to the learning process rather than the other way round, has had a very limited influence.

The Vocationalization of Senior Secondary School
In his speech at the National Conference on Education held in April, 1978, Deng Xiaoping stated that China had to train future workers who would be able to fulfil the demands of the economic modernization program, and that the country should therefore "...plan to increase the number of agricultural secondary schools and vocational and technical secondary schools".[8] This signaled fundamental changes in the monolithic structure of secondary education.

A number of arguments were put forward in the media to support the establishment of more vocational schools. First of all it was pointed out that China desperately needed skilled workers and middle level technicians. Secondly,

---

7. See, for example, the *Hong Qi* (*Red Flag*) articles translated in *Seybolt 1973*, pp. 229-246.

8. *Deng 1984*, p. 124.

the transition rate from senior secondary school to university was very low. As college enrolment could only be gradually expanded, it was considered a waste to keep so many students in general secondary schools as they, implicitly, did little else than prepare students for further education. Thirdly, China was facing a grave youth unemployment problem, which could be partly solved if more students received vocational training before leaving school.

There were, however, important ideological obstacles to be overcome before a vocational track could be established. Some people held the view that the new "double education system" was an exact copy of the "two track system" of capitalist countries, which they accused of separating future workers from future intellectuals and children of the ruling class from workers' children at an early stage. This critique was met by the reformers with two main arguments. One was that intellectuals, according to the revised class analysis, were members of the working class and not exploiters, and thus the separation of future manual workers from future intellectuals was fundamentally different from streaming in capitalist societies. The other argument admitted a superficial similarity between the Chinese and the capitalist educational systems. But, it then went on to explain that this was because a society's educational system reflects its level of economic development and is therefore to a large degree independent of the subjective will of individuals. The complexity of the production process in an industrialized society simply forces the educational system to divide students into different streams reflecting the division of labour. The vocationalization of secondary education was thus a manifestation of objective "laws" rather than a political choice.[9]

As the leaders had already decided to follow the vocationalization strategy, there was remarkably little theoretical debate on its relevance to China in the media in the late 1970s. There were reports about the state of vocational education in industrialized countries, which were regarded as models for China, but practically no research was published about the mixed results of vocationalization reforms in Third World countries.

Instead of a theoretical debate, practical experiments were carried out in several provinces and a number of different models were tried.[10] Already during

---

9. Both types of arguments are found, for example, in *RMJY* no. 12, 1979, p. 4-5. For an elaboration of the last argument, see *Cheng 1982*. The idea that certain objective laws should govern education and that it is the task of educational theory to discover these laws has been very popular in China after 1978. For a more detailed discussion, see *Brown 1982*.

10. A brief but interesting survey of the first steps of reform can be found in *Yunnan Jiaoyu* (*Yunnan Education*) no. 4, 1979, p. 9-10.

the first half of 1980 two national level meetings were held to discuss the first experiences with vocational middle schools and the future course of the reform, and a "*Report on the Reform of the Structure of Secondary Education*" was worked out. This report, which was confirmed by the State Council in October that year,[11] limited the scope of reform to senior secondary education, keeping the large majority of junior middle schools as general schools. It allowed not only the educational authorities, but also industrial organizations, enterprises, people's communes and even individuals to establish full-time, part-time and spare-time vocational schools, preferably in some kind of cooperative manner.

The report mentioned that one way to establish vocational schools should be to convert existing general schools. The remaining general schools should offer optional vocational courses. It was stressed that graduates from vocational middle schools, unlike those from specialized middle schools and workers' training schools (see below), would not be guaranteed a job by the state. On the other hand, they were, also unlike graduates from those other types of schools, free to take the university entrance examination. If they applied for further studies inside their own speciality, they would even be favoured over general school graduates. According to the report, special funds should be set aside locally for vocational education, but all schools should strive to become at least partly self-supporting. The proportion of vocational school students at the senior secondary level should be "largely increased", but the report did not dictate the exact proportion. With this report, the central authorities had provided a framework for the vocationalization of senior secondary education.

The reform was still in its initial phase, however. Statistics show that by 1981 there were only a few provinces where vocational and agricultural middle schools enrolled any considerable proportion of senior middle school students. Fifty-six percent of all vocational students were found in the three northeastern provinces of Jilin, Liaoning and Heilongjiang, which also enrolled 23% of all agricultural school students.[12] In other provinces vocational schools were concentrated only in a few cities, like Suzhou and Wuxi in Jiangsu. The vocationalization thus got the best start in areas, like Jiangsu province and the Northeast, with a solid industrial base and a tradition for vocational education.

It is worth noting that Jilin, which had been a model province in the field of education during the Cultural Revolution decade, was also in the forefront of the vocationalization process. This could indicate that some of the education-

---

11. *Zhongguo Jiaoyu Nianjian 1949-1981*, pp. 708-709.

12. *Zhongguo Jiaoyu Nianjian 1949-1981*, p. 183.

with-production policies of the Cultural Revolution did, in fact, provide a basis for the later expansion of vocational education. It is also interesting to note that there seems to be no connection between commitment to economic reform and reform of secondary education, as can be seen from the case of Sichuan province, where the first experiments with a more liberal economy were carried out, but where vocationalization started late.

In May, 1983, the Ministries of Education, Labour and Personnel and Finance together with the State Planning Commission jointly demanded that by 1990 around half of all students at the senior secondary level should be in vocational schools. They also called for a reform of the employment system that would force the enterprises to give preference in employment to those who had received relevant vocational training. This was seen as a pre-condition for the success of the vocationalization reform.[13]

From 1981 onwards, there was a considerable expansion in enrolment in secondary vocational education in almost all provinces. Table 8.1 shows how the four types of vocational schools gradually expanded their share of the total number of senior secondary school students from 23% in 1981 to 45% in 1988. The fastest expansion has taken place in the new vocational and agricultural middle schools, which in 1988 enrolled almost 47% of all vocational students as compared to only 22% in 1981.

In spite of this impressive expansion the central authorities were not satisfied with the results of the reform. The important "CCP Central Committee Decision on the Reform of the Educational Structure" of May, 1985, which was meant as a blueprint for the development of education, confirmed the vocationalization strategy but still called vocational and technical education "the weakest link in the whole field of education in our country". It repeated that the lack of emphasis on technical qualifications in the recruitment of new workers and employees was the main obstacle to the vocationalization of secondary education.[14]

In the summer of 1986, Li Peng, at that time vice premier and head of the State Education Commission, stated that the development of vocational education had been "uneven", and that rural areas in particular had been slow in implementing the reform. The emphasis should therefore still be on developing

---

13. Jiaoyubu, Laodong-Renshibu, Caizhengbu, Guojia Jiwei: "Guanyu gaige chengshi zhongdeng jiaoyu jiegou, fazhan zhiye jishu jiaoyu de yijian" (9 May, 1983). *Jiaoyu Gaige*, pp. 477-482.

14. "Zhonggong zhongyang guanyu jiaoyu tizhi gaige de jueding", 27 May, 1985. *Jiaoyu Gaige*, pp 15-28.

rather than consolidating the different types of vocational schools, which at this time already enrolled 36% of all senior secondary school students.[15]

Ever since Deng Xiaoping's speech at the work conference in 1978, China has thus stuck to the vocationalization strategy. However, vocational education is still seen as a "weak link" in the educational system. Before entering into a more detailed discussion of the problems surrounding vocational education, however, a brief presentation of the main types of secondary vocational schools will be given.

Four Types of Vocational Secondary Schools

There are four major kinds of vocational schools at the secondary level: vocational middle schools, agricultural middle schools, workers' training schools and specialized middle schools. The following description is based partly on visits to such institutions in Beijing and Yantai, Shandong in 1984 and in Harbin, Heilongjiang 1986 and 1987, and partly on reports published by the Chinese media.

Vocational middle schools (VMS) (zhiye zhongxue)

This has been the fastest expanding type of vocational school in the period after 1978. Most of these schools have been converted from general middle schools, and former general school teachers make up most of the staff. Some general middle schools have established vocational classes, where the students receive the same type of training as in VMS.

Training objectives. When the first VMS were established after 1978, their training objectives and position in the educational system were not very clear, and the choice of specialities offered in each school often depended on what its teachers felt qualified to teach, rather than on the actual need of the local community for qualified manpower. The Chinese authorities gradually realized, however, that the most promising future for the VMS lay in the training of workers and other staff for the rapidly developing service sector, where the work force lacked formal training opportunities. In Beijing, 90% of all VMS students were enrolled in specialities leading to non-manual jobs or jobs in "tertiary production", i.e. the service sector, in 1986.[16] In other areas industrial specialities play

---

15. Li Peng: "Dali fazhan zhiye jishu jiaoyu shi jiaoyu gaige de zhongyao neirong" (To develop vocational and technical education is an important aspect of educational reform), 30 August, 1986. *Jiaoyu Gaige*, pp. 338-350.

16. *Quanguo Zhiye 1986*, p. 114.

a much greater role. The following main types of specialities are offered in VMS:

1: Specialities aiming at such non-manual professions as kindergarten teachers, accountants or medical workers, where the work force has traditionally been composed of a small number of people trained in specialized middle schools and a much larger number who have only received general education.

2: Specialities related to industry, like welding, bench work or printing. These specialities often overlap courses offered at workers' training schools.

3: Specialities related to handicrafts and repair work, like tailoring, watch repairing or TV repairing, where the work force was traditionally trained in more or less formalized apprenticeship programs.

4: Specialities related to building and construction, for example brick-laying and carpentry, where the work force was traditionally rural and received little formal education.

5: "High tech" specialities, particularly in the computer field, where job prospects are expected to be good, and where the older types of schools are unable to fill the demand.

6: Specialities related to agriculture, particularly to sideline productions in the suburban villages, like vegetable growing and aquaculture.

Organization. Some schools are run by a local government's education department, and a smaller number are run by enterprises. The kind of organization recommended by the State Education Commission, however, is one of joint administration between an enterprise or a local government's industrial department on one side and an education department on the other. This arrangement normally implies that the educational authorities provide buildings, all general subject and some vocational subject teachers and part of the running expenses, while the enterprise contributes some vocational subject teachers, training facilities, equipment and supplementary funds. The enterprise also normally hires all or most of the qualified graduates.

VMS are markedly cheaper than other types of vocational education. The annual cost per student is only around one third of that of the workers' training schools.[17]

Teachers. The teaching force can be divided into general and vocational subject teachers. As most VMS are former general middle schools, the general

---

17. *Jihua Jingji Yanjiu (Research in Planned Economy)* no. 10, 1982, pp. 32-36.

subject teachers are usually easily recruited among the teachers of the original general school. The majority of vocational subject teachers are also former general school teachers, who either teach a subject within their original field (like a physics teacher teaching electronics) or have received some extra training. Some technicians function as part-time teachers, particularly in enterprise-run schools, and a small number of graduates of technical colleges are assigned jobs as VMS teachers. Finally, a number of cities have established special training institutes for vocational school teachers, in some cases with aid from the World Bank. It is often difficult, however, to find teachers for the vocational courses, partly because these teaching jobs hold low social prestige.

Student recruitment. All students who graduate from junior middle school can take the annual examinations for the different types of schools at the senior secondary level. In the early 1980s, VMS were almost always students' third or fourth choice, and consequently only those with the lowest scores entered these schools. This pattern now seems to be changing, at least in some areas. In 1987, for example, I was told that many VMS in Harbin required a higher admission score than general schools. According to the authorities, the improvement of job prospects for VMS graduates has increased the prestige of the VMS. It was easier for them to find jobs than for general school graduates, and they furthermore do not have to go through apprenticeship training before getting a regular job. A recent Chinese survey carried out in Xi'an and Canton likewise shows that the popularity of the VMS mainly depends on job prospects: a more lively economy with a relatively more flexible job structure creates a greater demand for VMS graduates.[18]

A special restriction on VMS is that only students with an urban household registration can be enrolled.[19] This rule is, of course, one of the means used by the government to control rural-urban migration. If rural students were accepted by the VMS, they might later get a job in an urban enterprise and achieve the much-coveted urban status.

Curriculum and Teaching. The ratio between the time devoted to general and to vocational subjects in VMS is 1:1, with increasing emphasis on vocational subjects towards the end of the course. In Harbin's No. 1 Girls' Vocational Senior Middle School, for example, vocational subjects took up 30% the first year, 40% the second year and 70% the third year. A considerable part of the time spent on vocational subjects (two thirds in one school I visited), is devoted

---

18. *JYYJ* no. 1, 1988, pp 42-45.

19. *Zhongguo Jiaoyu Nianjian 1949-1981*, p. 185.

to basic theory related to the speciality, which leaves little time for practical training.

Employment. As mentioned above, the crucial factor for the future of the VMS is probably job prospects. While the two other types of vocational schools at the senior secondary level are normally able to guarantee all of their graduates a job inside the privileged state owned sector, VMS do not offer such a guarantee. They are thus part of the reform of the job system leading away from lifelong employment (the so-called "iron rice-bowl" system) and job allocation by the state, towards a more market-oriented system. According to the Harbin Education Commission, around 80% of the city's 1987 VMS graduates found jobs within the first two months after graduation. This was markedly better than in previous years, and presumably also better than the situation for general middle school students. Some cities, like Beijing, have reported even higher employment rates,[20] but as the Harbin authorities were quite proud of their 80% rate, and as the employment problem is often mentioned in local reports on VMS, it can be taken for granted that the problem of finding jobs for VMS graduates has not yet been completely solved.

Agricultural middle schools (AMS) (nongye zhongxue)

Agricultural middle schools are very similar to VMS, and in the statistics, these two types of schools are often counted together. The main differences are that AMS are established in rural areas, enroll rural students and primarily teach specialities related to agriculture.

Training objectives. Though broad, traditional specializations like grain production or animal husbandry are common in AMS, it is the aim of many schools to qualify their students to set up "specialized households" (*zhuanye hu*), which can earn money through some sort of specialized production. For this purpose courses in 52 different specializations were offered in Chinese AMS already in 1981.[21] AMS thus fit into the plan for a diversification and specialization of Chinese agriculture.

Organization. Some schools are run by the counties, other by lower levels. Many of them are in very poor condition, as it was almost always the low-quality general middle schools which were converted into AMS. In 1984, I visited the only county-run AMS in Laiyang county, Shandong province. The material conditions here were far more primitive than what I had seen in the nearby city

---

20. *Quanguo Zhiye 1986*, pp. 116.

21. A list of these specialities can be found in *Zhongguo Jiaoyu Nianjian 1949-1981*, p. 184.

of Yantai. The school buildings had thatched roofs and clay floors, and doors and windows could not be shut tight. In the dormitory, sixteen students shared a room of around 25 square meters. Still this school was considered one of the best AMS in Yantai district, and even the district itself is rich by Chinese standards.

Teachers are a particular problem in AMS, because it is very difficult to find people with both theoretical and practical qualifications who are willing to work as teachers in these low-prestige schools. Part-time teachers are therefore often employed.

Student recruitment. AMS have held even lower prestige than their urban counterparts (the VMS) and have been treated as second-rate institutions by authorities, parents and students alike. This tendency was strongest during the first years of reform. By 1984, some Yantai AMS required a higher admission score than general schools, though not as high, of course, as the one required by key schools. It seems that AMS became more popular as rural students realized that the examination system gave them very few chances of entering university. In most areas, however, students still prefer to go to a general school, and the lack of applicants for AMS has been one of the main reasons why the vocationalization reform has progressed rather slowly in rural areas.

Curriculum and teaching. In principle, students' time is divided evenly between general and vocational subjects. The Laiyang county AMS had experimental fields and other production facilities where students could put their knowledge into practice. Often, however, the principle of half-work-half-study is employed in the AMS. This means that students in schools of lower quality go to school only part of the day or year to study part of the general school curriculum, while they spend the rest of their time in the fields with work not necessarily related to what they are studying in school, just as earlier generations of rural youth have done ever since the 1950s. AMS were, in fact, in the initial phase of the reform period, accused of being a product of Cultural Revolution ideas because students did so much manual work.

Employment. The authorities have no obligation to find jobs for AMS graduates. Some of them find work as basic level agricultural technicians, AMS teachers or tractor drivers, while the majority go to work on the family land.

Workers' training schools (WTS) (gongren jishu xuexiao)
Compared to VMS, workers' training schools are more like Soviet-type institutions as they have a close relationship to industrial enterprises and narrow technical specialities.

Training objectives. WTS train skilled workers for jobs in industry, mainly in traditional industrial specializations like welding, milling, lathe work etc.... Workers with a WTS background start out as primary level workers (grades 1-3 on the eight-grade scale on which all workers are placed), but are expected to advance to the medium level (grades 4-6).

Organization. The Ministry of Labour supervises these schools and approves curriculum plans etc..., which means that they lie outside the control of the education sector authorities. The real power, however, lies with the organs that fund them, i.e. central or provincial industrial departments or enterprises. Schools are partly financed through the students' productive labour. Their economic dependency on a single enterprise can be a problem, particularly after the introduction of the market-oriented industrial reforms. The leaders of the Weijian Factory's WTS in Harbin, for example, complained that they were unable to buy new equipment, because the factory made little profit at the moment on its production of aeroplanes.

Teachers. Most WTS teachers are skilled workers, technicians or engineers from the enterprise or department running the school. In general, they are thus technically qualified, but have normally received very little, if any, pedagogical training. WTS appear to be overstaffed, with only four students per staff member compared to almost ten in vocational middle schools.[22] One reason why China decided to start up vocational middle schools instead of further developing the existing WTS is probably exactly the low cost-efficiency of the latter type of school.

Student recruitment. Students enter WTS via an entrance examination after either junior or senior middle school. During the first half of the 1980s, most of the students enrolled were senior middle school graduates unable to find employment. Now, however, it is the official aim to reduce the number of senior middle school graduates enrolled in order to make WTS an alternative to general senior secondary school rather than a continuation of it. In 1987, the WTS had only 1.9 million students following the two-year courses, which are normally held for senior middle school graduates, against 8.4 mill. in three-years courses for junior middle school graduates.[23] WTS is thus becoming a viable alternative within senior secondary education.

In spite of an officially exam-based admission procedure, a large part of the students in the WTS I visited were children of the enterprises' own workers

---

22. *Zhongguo Tongji Nianjian 1988*, pp. 874, 876, 888.

23. *Zhongguo Tongji Nianjian 1988*, p. 888.

and staff. This is partly due to family traditions, but it is also because many schools still enroll students through the replacement system (*dingti*), which guarantees workers' children the right to inherit their parents' job when they retire. This system has been under heavy fire from the central authorities for years, as it stands in sharp contrast to all meritocratic principles, but it seems to be very hard to abolish.

Curriculum and training. The curriculum consists of around one-half classroom teaching and one-half practical work. In class, around 60% of the time is spent on skill-related theory (physics, chemistry, etc...), while 20% is spent on more narrowly specialized technical disciplines and 20% on general subjects (like politics and Chinese, for example). Practical training is carried out either in a school factory or at the hosting enterprise. This training is of a productive character and contributes to the financing of the school.

Employment. After graduation, WTS students have traditionally been assigned to a permanent position in the enterprise or department to which their school belonged. In theory, this system has been under change in the late 1980s, and students are supposed to gradually start finding their own jobs.[24] In reality, however, little seems to have changed so far. Almost all 1986 Harbin WTS graduates, for example, were allocated jobs in state-owned enterprises, and as far as I know, no complaints have been heard from WTS graduates about difficulties in finding employment.

Specialized middle schools (SMS) (zhongdeng zhuanye xuexiao)
This type of school ranks highest in prestige among secondary level vocational schools. Like the WTS, they have their roots in the period of close cooperation with the Soviet Union in the 1950s.

Training objectives. SMS train middle level technicians and "white collar" staff. Most graduates receive cadre status. Table 8.2 shows the distribution of students by major field of study. Teachers' training schools, which have lost some ground compared to other specializations but still enroll one third of all students in SMS, educate primary school teachers. Health sector schools mainly train hospital nurses and laboratory workers, while schools in finance and economics train people like accountants for industrial enterprises. Industrial schools train middle level technicians.

---

24. This intention is expressed, for example, in the main report from the National Work Conference on Vocational and Technical Education held in 1986. See *Quanguo Zhiye 1986*, pp. 24-32.

Organization. The State Education Commission is responsible for the curricula of all SMS, but only directly run the teachers' training schools. Other schools are run by sectoral (health, light industry etc...) departments at the national, provincial or city government level. In 1985, 295 schools were run by organs at the national level, 1,207 by the provinces and 1,027 by lower levels.[25]

Teachers. With a student/staff ratio of 4.3 to one in 1988,[26] SMS are amply if not over-staffed. Most schools have a competent teaching force with an adequate theoretical background. In 1986, 48% of all SMS teachers had four years of university education behind them (*benke biye*), while 25% had received a three year college education (*zhuanke biye*).[27]

Student recruitment. Like WTS, SMS are meant to change their focus of recruitment from senior to junior middle school graduates, but have been much slower in doing so, because SMS in the minds of many Chinese are placed somewhere between senior secondary and tertiary education. In 1986, two thirds of all new entrants in Harbin's SMS still came from senior middle school, and those who came directly from junior middle school were mostly enrolled in the health and education sector schools, which have always enrolled this type of students. Most industrial schools, on the other hand, still exclusively enrolled senior middle school graduates. In 1987 I was told that this situation was rapidly changing. One reason, however, is probably that many of the best SMS have been upgraded to "specialized colleges" (*zhuanke xuexiao*) and have thus disappeared from the statistics of secondary education.

Curriculum and teaching. The period of schooling is normally two years for senior and four years for junior middle school graduates. The curricula are centrally planned and characterized by a high degree of specialization, particularly in industrial subjects. In 1981, for example, there were 242 industrial specialities, out of which 64 were within the machine industry alone.[28] Students are placed in classes according to speciality from the first term, and though part of the curriculum is common to several specialities, there is little chance of changing one's field of study later on. Practical training takes up from one fourth to one third of the curriculum and is conducted either in school factories and laboratories or in enterprises and institutions.

---

25. *Quanguo Zhiye 1986*, p. 417.

26. *Zhongguo Tongji Nianjian 1989*, pp. 817, 818.

27. *Quanguo Zhiye 1986*, p. 415.

28. *Zhongguo Jiaoyu Nianjian 1949-1981*, pp. 214-217 contains a list of all specialities.

Employment. The same change towards a more market-oriented employment system which was mentioned for the WTS, is planned to take place in the SMS. Again, however, figures from Harbin showed that almost all graduates were still being employed in state-owned enterprises. There is very little information about how the job allocation system actually works, but the school's power to decide the future fate of its students has traditionally been an important disciplining factor. One commercial school visited in 1987 had, however, abolished the closed-door policy in favour of a transparent and purely meritocratic system: After the final examination, all posts which according to the plan should be filled with graduates from a particular class, were listed on the blackboard. The students were then allowed, in the order of their score on the final examination, to choose which job they wanted.

Problems In Vocational Education
As mentioned above, the vocationalization reform has run into a number of problems during the last ten years. The fast expansion has led to a severe shortage of qualified teachers. Many schools, particularly the new VMS and AMS, but also the more established schools, have very limited funds, mainly because local leaders have preferred to invest in directly productive activities rather than in education and training. Teaching materials have been of low quality. It has been very difficult to adapt vocational training to the demands of the employers. And it has proved difficult to "sell" vocational education to students and their parents, who often have held the traditional view that general education is the only genuine kind of education. All these problems are a natural consequence of China's position as a relatively poor Third World country with a weak tradition for vocational education.

Considering that many of the problems were quite predictable, it is remarkable that there has been so little debate in China on the relative advantages of vocational and general education. China started the vocationalization reform because of its shortage of skilled workers and middle level technicians and it no doubt needed these kinds of manpower in 1978 and still does today. With this perspective the expanded enrolment in vocational education appears to be a wise and inevitable policy. It is worth noting, however, that international experiences with vocational training in secondary schools are far from rosy, particularly when we look at countries in the Third World. W. Norton Grubb has surveyed the literature on this subject:

A finding common to many countries is that, despite claims of economic "relevance", vocationalized approaches prove to have little economic justification, fail to resolve the problems that they are designed to address, and generate new problems for education systems.[29]

Even the World Bank, which has supported the vocationalization strategy and involved itself in projects in this field in China, displayed considerable scepticism in its 1985 report on Chinese education:

> The experience of other countries in implementing vocationalization programs has been mixed. Several shortcomings have often (but not always) been observed in systems that provide vocational education, particularly in industrial skills, in schools.... On the other hand graduates of vocational programs generally possess stronger academic background than those who enter the workforce without secondary education and are often more able to adjust to the changing work requirements including the introduction of new technology or promotion to assignments demanding more advanced knowledge as well as skills....
>
> While the results [in other countries] tend to show that the relatively high costs of formal technical and vocational education are not associated with correspondingly higher benefits, in terms of increased worker productivity, by comparison, say, with general education or on-the-job training, the findings are not easily generalized.... Despite planning of major new investments in Chinese technical and vocational education, it appears that research into these questions in China is not yet complete.[30]

The essence of these remarks seems to be that vocational education at this level is better than no education, but that its advantage lies in the general qualifications acquired, not in the specific skills. The main reason is, of course, that it is very difficult to match the skills taught in schools with the qualification needs of the employers. Furthermore, these needs change with technological development, which means that vocational skills become obsolete more quickly than general qualifications.

This raises two questions: Why did the Chinese leaders, before carrying out substantial research on the relative merits of vocational and general middle school education, take it for granted that vocational training inside the school system was the solution to the problem of the insufficient supply of skilled

---

29. *Grubb 1985*, p. 256.

30. *World Bank 1985*, pp. 28-29.

manpower; and why have the international experiences presented and discussed in the Chinese media the last ten years been those of the Federal Republic of Germany and other industrialized countries rather than those of developing countries whose situation more closely resembled China's? The main answer to the last question is that China's opening up to the outside world, as mentioned in Chapter 3, has primarily been an opening to the industrialized West. The reform leaders' image of China as a country on its way to rapid modernization has made the experiences of poor African and Asian countries seem irrelevant. To answer the first question, however, it is necessary to look at the reduced role of practical work in general middle schools after 1978.

Theory and Practice In General Schools
The following discussion on the relationship between "theoretical" learning, i.e. book learning, and practical training in general secondary schools takes as its starting point my impression of the teaching process in one second year senior middle school class at Beijing Normal University's No. 2. Attached Middle School during one week in the spring of 1984. I choose this angle, because these few days gave me a more vivid impression of the actual teaching methods used in Chinese schools than many articles in educational magazines had done. It should be noted that the No. 2 Attached is one of the absolute elite schools in the country and that its teachers are considered to be of top quality. What I met was therefore not a group of teachers who were, for some reason, unable to live up to official standards, but rather a showcase of Chinese teaching at its very best.

A week in a general senior middle school
The school day started at 7·45 in the morning with self study in the classroom. At 8:00 the regular lessons began, continuing until around 4:00 pm, interrupted at noon by a two hour lunch break. Except for two weekly lessons of physical education and the radio exercises every morning, all time was occupied by theoretical subjects with an emphasis on the natural sciences.

There was little variation in teaching method. The teachers followed the textbooks quite strictly. This was necessary because the textbook contained exactly what the students had to learn in order to pass the university entrance examination.

The content of what was taught was very rarely connected to the outside world. Abstract principles of natural sciences were explained by the teacher and understood, or memorized, by the students, but there was little discussion of how the principles were utilized in production. As a sign of its key school status, this school had laboratories for physics, chemistry and biology, but their capacity was insufficient, and most lessons in these subjects had to be taught in an ordinary classroom. In a subject like politics the situation appeared even worse. I heard the teacher go through Mao's famous article "On Practice" without so much as once relating the text to any phenomenon outside the realm of philosophy. The students were asked to learn the definition of "social practice" by heart without any reflections over the glaring contrast between this teaching method and the content of the text.

The students had some practical tasks, like keeping their classroom in order, but these were totally unrelated to the content of teaching. They should have, according to the curriculum, engaged in productive labour two weeks each semester, but this rule was not taken very seriously. In the spring semester of 1984 the participation in productive labour was reduced to one Saturday, when students helped plant trees around the school buildings and prepared the sports ground for a sports festival. In their spare time the boarding students stayed at school, while the others went home or took part in extracurricular activities, where sports were a popular choice. They spent the rest of the day doing their homework or preparing for one of the tests which would inevitably turn up during the week. All in all they had very little time for contact with the outside world.

Officially, the principle of education-with-production has never been abandoned in general secondary education. According to the 1978 instructional plan, students in junior and senior middle school should take part in productive labour for five and seven weeks a year respectively, and the teaching of physics, to mention just one example, should stress the application of physical principles in production.[31] Though the annual participation in productive labour in junior and senior middle school was cut down to two and four weeks respectively in 1981, there was no change of principle, and in October, 1982 the Ministry of Education issued rather detailed guidelines for labour education, praising all its political, moral and pedagogical advantages.[32] At the same time, the part-work-part-study program of Jilin province, which had been a pace-setter in this field, was praised at a national conference, and its principles were promoted all over

---

31. *Zhongguo Jiaoyu Nianjian 1949-1981*, pp. 472-73.

32. *RMJY* no. 1, 1983, pp 27-28.

the country.[33] In 1987 a teaching program for labour education was published suggesting which practical skills students should learn in each year of junior and senior middle school, from woodwork and clothes washing in junior first to the repair of agricultural machinery in senior third year.[34]

There have also been reports of pedagogical experiments where the content of study has been related to local conditions and to production needs. Many of these experiments seem to have taken place in rural areas where the contrast between a curriculum totally geared towards the needs of those trying to get access to tertiary education on the one hand and the extremely small proportion of students who ever make it that far in the educational system on the other must have been the most striking. There have been reports of general middle schools in Jiangsu, for instance, trying to adapt the content of education to the needs of the villages by teaching about chemical fertilizers in chemistry classes, about agricultural machinery in physics classes and so on.[35] In Guangdong plans have been announced to devote 20% of class time to vocational and technical subjects in non-key general middle schools and 10% in key schools. It was argued that such lessons not only provide students with vocational skills but also benefit their general intellectual development.[36]

However, such experiments are still exceptions. Keith M. Lewin has analyzed the post-reform science curriculum in Chinese schools and found that it is "characterized by subject specialization, emphasis on the physical sciences, infrequent practical activity by students, emphasis on content rather than process skills, and theoretical rather than applied approaches to the subject matter".[37] This characterization could (except for the second point) be applied to cultural and social science subjects as well.

The large majority of articles and reports in Chinese educational magazines confirm this opinion: Post Mao Chinese middle schools, in spite of paying occasional lip service to the principle of combining education with labour, have been totally dominated by book learning while neglecting its practical application and students have had little contact with the outside world in general and

33. *Quanguo Zhongxiaoxue 1982* contains documents and reports on part-work-part-study programs in a number of localities.

34. *RMJY* no. 7-8, 1987, pp. 11-12, 30.

35. *Jiangsu Jiaoyu (Jiangsu Education)* no. 5, 1983, pp. 2-3.

36. *Guangdong Jiaoyu (Guangdong Education)* no. 8, 1982, p. 6.

37. *Lewin 1987*, pp. 430-431.

with the world of production in particular. The situation can be summed up in the following description from a 1988 *Educational Research* article:

> In the last years,...labour education has, in reality, basically been abolished in general primary and secondary school. The phenomenon of students looking down upon labour and on the labouring people is very serious. When they graduate from secondary school, they are not only ideologically unprepared for taking part in productive work, they are also unprepared in regard to knowledge, skills and habits.[38]

Education-With-Production - A Discussion

Returning to the four main aspects of the education-with-production concept - the moral-political, the economic, the pedagogical and the vocational - we find that the *moral-political* idea of implanting students with a socialist consciousness by letting them take part in productive labour survived the post-Mao reforms. It appears in instructional plans, in the speeches of leading cadres and in some ritual remnants of labour education in general middle schools all through the period. In reality, however, very little time has been spent on such activities, and they have had no substantial influence on the ideology of middle school students; the hidden curriculum has taught them that passing the examinations is what really matters.

The part-work-part-study programs, however, have not lost their importance, because the *economic* motives for students' participation in production still exist. As mentioned in Chapter 5, the economic responsibility for secondary education in rural areas rests mainly with local authorities, who generally encourage students' participation in productive labour because it helps cover the cost of running the schools. In some cases however, the economic aspect is used as an argument for keeping the students away from production. In many of the urban and some of the rural schools which I visited, the work in the school work shops and factories was not done by students but by ordinary workers. Some of these workers were former students of the same schools, who had been unable to find other jobs. In one case, many of the workers were children of the school's teachers and staff, who saw this arrangement as a sort of "fringe benefit". The profits of the school work shops were reported to rise when the students were excluded from the work place, because the "real" workers were much more efficient. The replacement of student labour with ordinary workers is, perhaps, the

---

38. *JYYJ* no. 2, 1988, pp. 19-21 (p. 19).

most evident example of the importance attached to the economic aspect of the education-with-production concept.

The *pedagogical* aspect seems to have received the least attention of the four. This is certainly true for the general middle schools, as mentioned above. But it is even true for vocational education, where the integration of basic theory, speciality-related theory and practical training has been a big problem in all three types of schools.

The *vocational* aspect has constantly been underlined: Secondary education should prepare students for their future occupation and provide them with the practical skills of a trade. It should be noted, however, that vocational education has spread very slowly in the *junior* section of secondary school. As mentioned in Chapter 6, only around 15% of the age cohort receive senior secondary education, so even when half of these students are in the vocational track the overwhelming majority of young Chinese will still leave the educational system without having received any vocational training. Experiments have been carried out with adding an extra year of vocational training to junior middle school (the 5+4+3 system, cf. Chapter 5), but this is still an exception.

If we now return to the question of why China threw itself into a vocationalization reform without conducting a substantial theoretical debate and without much consideration of the mixed results of such strategies in other developing contries, an answer may be found in the larger context of the whole educational reform process, and in particular in the reintroduction of the examination system. As shown above, practical work almost totally disappeared from Chinese secondary schools after the reintroduction of the university entrance examinations. This happened because the form and content of the examinations called for rote learning of abstract knowledge rather than the application of theoretical knowledge to practical problems. Education thus became irrelevant for the majority of students, who knew that they would be unable to pass the entrance examination. Given the impossibility of combining theoretical learning with practical work in any meaningful way in the general middle schools, vocationalization became the only way to maintain an already severely damaged contact between secondary education and the world of production. The really noteworthy point about the connection between education and production in the post-Mao secondary education is thus not the establishment of vocational schools but the inability of the reformers to design a curriculum capable of transmitting useful general and specific skills to the large majority of the students.

This point is most clearly demonstrated by the rural schools. It is striking how recent criticisms of rural education resemble, not in form but in content,

Cultural Revolution attacks on what was called, in the more militant language of that time, "Liu Shaoqi's black line in education". In mid-1986, for example, a Shanxi official declared, after describing the miserable condition of rural secondary education following the introduction of entrance examinations:

> We must add some agricultural knowledge to the textbooks used in the last years of primary school and in secondary school, so that the students know a bit about what is going on around them in agricultural production....At present, the large majority of rural middle school students want to....leave the countryside. If schools provided them with some basic skills that would enable them to change the backward conditions of their village fewer people would want to leave...[39]

Other writers equally familiar with the situation in rural schools have pointed out, subject by subject, how the content of the textbooks used is totally out of touch with students' lives and needs and therefore also very difficult for the students to comprehend.[40] The establishment of agricultural middle schools only solves this problem at the senior secondary level and only for some of the students.

In the eyes of the reformers, the vocational middle schools have a number of advantages. In urban areas, they fulfil a useful role in training manpower for jobs at the medium skill-level. They also take some of the pressure off the examination system, as few vocational school graduates sign up for the university entrance examination, which they would have very poor chances of passing anyway. This means that the admittance ratio has increased, while the number of frustrated and dissatisfied young people has dropped.

Furthermore, vocational middle schools are all in accordance with the economic reforms. They train people for the expanding service sector, for small scale industries and for the specialized households in the villages. Moreover, as opposed to the graduates of specialized middle schools and workers' training schools, the graduates of vocational middle schools are not automatically guaranteed a job. They have to go to enterprises and apply for one, and thereby become the spearheads of a new employment system based on market mechanisms and competition rather than on state allocation and plans. Vocational middle schools have also become an alternative road of mobility into the ranks of the skilled workers, a road which is outside the control of the enterprises and of the

---

39. *RMJY* no. 7/8, 1986, p. 14.

40. *RMJY* no. 11, 1986, p. 11.

existing powerful stratum of state-employed craftsmen. This will help to break the monopoly of the offspring of this stratum on skilled jobs and to soften up the rigid employment system.

In spite of these advantages, however, the vocationalization strategy has not solved the problem of how to combine education with production in general schools, or how to make education relevant for the later working life of the large majority of students. These questions are still unanswered, particularly in rural middle schools, and the pressure for answers is growing.

One way to strengthen applied knowledge, practical skills and vocational preparation in middle school could be to strengthen vocational and agricultural education in *junior* middle schools. Suggestions have been put forward about establishing a vocational track in both urban and rural junior secondary education,[41] but most debaters concentrate on the rural schools. Again, however, the question is whether practical skills and manual labour should be part of the education of all students or whether a separate vocational track should be established. Early streaming may well lead to popular discontent, while more emphasis on vocational subjects for all rural students would make them less competitive than their urban counterparts at the entrance examinations for senior middle school. Unfortunately, the most likely thing to happen after the student demonstrations in 1989 is that the moral-political aspect of labour education will be re-emphasized. If labour education now again is to be used as a sort of punishment, its prestige will drop even lower, and it will become even more difficult to bring into play the pedagogical aspect of the concept.

We shall now turn from technical to ideological qualifications. In Chapter 7, we saw how the selective and elite-oriented middle school system created intense competition among the students, a feeling of superiority among the winners and low self-esteem among the losers. At the same time, students' respect for labour and for the labouring classes, one of the cardinal virtues of Communist ethics, has deteriorated through the reform decade. Moral education, the topic of Chapter 9, is intended to redress such undesired effects of the reforms.

---

41. Xu Hai: "Shi tan cheng-xiang chuzhong jiayuo fenliu wenti" (Tentative remarks on the streaming of urban and rural secondary education), *RMJY* no. 10, 1988, pp. 20-21.

9. Moral Education

The Chinese concept of "moral education" (*deyu*) covers the teaching of politics, ideology and morality to students in a planned and organized way, not only through the educational system but also through the family and other agents, such as the Communist Youth League.[1] This chapter will first examine the ideological qualifications transmitted to middle school students as a part of the conscious teaching/learning process. Secondly, we shall discuss the clash between the norms and values transmitted in moral education on one hand and the hidden curriculum of the schools as well as other social realities facing Chinese students in the 1980s on the other hand. Finally, we shall turn to what the Chinese authorities conceive to be the problems in middle school students' ideology during the reform decade.

The Politics Course

The hard core of moral education in Chinese secondary schools is the politics course, to which two weekly lessons are devoted in the junior as well as in the senior section. In 1981, a discussion draft of a teaching outline for this subject was published, and this provides a description of the course as it has been taught in middle schools during most of the reform decade.[2]

According to this outline, the theme of the *first year of junior middle school* was "the moral self-cultivation (*xiuyang*) of young people". It covers morality in a broad sense, from rules of proper behaviour to the establishment of "high ideals". The first part of the course should teach the students to love the nation, the people, the Party, science, labour and the collective and to respect teachers, parents and public morality, in other words teach them loyalty to the most important institutions of Chinese society. The second part should stress the development of cardinal virtues such as sincerity and humility, diligence and

---

1. For a closer definition see *Jiaoyu Cidian 1987*, p. 824-25.

2. The following discussion is based on the "Teaching Outlines for Secondary School Political Studies". All references are to the translation of this text in *CE*, vol. 16, no. 1, pp. 12-69, though I have changed the translation of some terms. This volume of *Chinese Education* also contains translations of other articles on political education.

frugality, optimism and revolutionary heroism. One important method of instruction is to set up models for the students so that they can "emulate those progressive people who have made outstanding contributions to the socialist enterprise" (p. 15).[3]

The theme of the *junior second year* as described in the outline is "General Knowledge of the Law".[4] This is an introduction not only to the constitution and criminal law but also to Chinese political and legal institutions such as the People's Congresses and to the fundamental rights of Chinese citizens.

In theory, students should learn to "analyze and solve problems on their own" (p. 28). This should not, however, be confused with the encouragement of an open debate of the fundamental issues:

> As yet undetermined issues should not be included in the teaching content, because junior middle school students have not yet attained, or lack, the capacity to distinguish clearly between right and wrong in theoretical issues. In organizing the teaching content, it is necessary that it agrees with the views of the Party on policy and on carrying out the law" (pp. 25-26).

The *junior third year* course is titled "A Brief History of Social Development". It introduces elementary Marxist-Leninist theory, first of all historical materialism and the theory of the five evolutionary stages of human society.

In the *senior section* there are courses in two other main aspects of Marxism-Leninism, i.e. the political economy of capitalist societies and dialectic materialism. In the senior section a more open attitude is recommended:

> Pay attention to the encouraging of a democratic atmosphere and to developing students' own initiative... Permit students to express their own differing opinions. Uphold the "three non-dogmatisms" of not labelling people, not dragging them by the hair, and not beating them (p. 62).

The aim of the whole politics course in middle school according to the discussion draft published in 1981 is thus twofold. It should implant students with the Chinese version of socialist morality on one hand, and propagate the CCP's view

---

3. For a discussion of the role of models in Chinese primary school textbooks, see *Ridley et al. 1971*.

4. The course was originally named 'General Knowledge of Politics' in Sept. 1980, but the name was changed when the outline appeared in 1981, probably under influence of the legalization wave in Chinese political life at the moment, cf. *Zhongguo Jiaoyu Nianjian 1949-1981*, p. 434.

on Marxist theory and on contemporary political questions on the other. For the latter purpose, students have since 1983 studied the works of Deng Xiaoping,[5] which have, to some degree, replaced Mao Zedong's works as canonical texts.

The politics course outlined in 1981 never succeeded in raising the interest of the students. In the many surveys made on students' preferences among different school subjects during the 1980s, politics has almost invariably been at the bottom of the list. One survey found that only 3.3% of the students listed politics as their favorite course, while 24.7% of them disliked it more than any other course.[6] According to another survey, students found that the teaching materials used in the politics course were empty and abstract, that "the teacher monopolizes the class and monologizes from beginning to end", and that "the method of examination is mechanical and rigid".[7]

This obvious distaste for the politics course has greatly worried CCP authorities, and several reforms have been attempted. One problem is, as mentioned above, that the content of the course has been far too abstract for the students. Marx's theory of the five stages of the evolution of human society, for example, cannot possibly raise much interest, let alone discussion, among sixteen-year-old youngsters, who can do little else with this theory than memorize it and reproduce it at the examination. Therefore the content of the course was changed in what should be a more practical, fact-oriented direction in 1986. At the same time, the titles of the courses, listed from junior first year to senior third year, were changed into the following: "Citizen Knowledge", "A Brief History of Social Development", "General Knowledge of Socialist Construction", "Communist Outlook On Life", "General Knowledge of Economy" and "General Knowledge of Politics".[8] The title af the subject was changed to "Ideology and Politics", instead of just "Politics". Despite adjustments, the central authorities have thus unwaveringly insisted on maintaining the moral/political aspect of the curriculum. The content of educational magazines actually shows an increasing attention being paid to moral education by the top leaders up through the 1980s.

Some middle school teachers have had ambitions of increasing the popularity of the course by making it a forum for genuine open debate between teachers and students on important moral, social and political issues. One teacher,

---

5. *Zhongguo Jiaoyu Nianjian 1982-1984*, p.92.

6. *JYYJ* no. 8, 1983, pp. 58-63, translated, together with other surveys on students' attitudes, in *CE*, vol. 17, no. 4, winter 1984-85.

7. *CE*, vol 17, no. 4, pp 72-73.

8. *RMJY* no. 7-8, 1987, pp. 26-27.

for example, suggested in an article in *People's Education* that the students be allowed to ask such questions as "Isn't the democracy of our nation really a fake" or "Are all people in China really equal before the law?". He argues that the teacher should discuss with the students on equal terms and on the basis of experiences from real life.[9] After the suppression of the student's movement in June 1989, it seems highly unlikely that any teacher will plunge into such high risk discussions. Even in the more liberal political climate earlier in the 1980s it was very difficult to change the content of the politics course in the direction of open discussion. This was partly because only orthodox answers were accepted on the politics test in the university entrance examination. But the most important reason was that the CCP, as mentioned in Chapter 3, has not given up its monopoly of power. As long as the CCP maintains that its views are always "correct", discussion can only be used as an instrument to bring about public support for these views.

Moral Education Outside the Politics Course

The transmission of ideological qualifications is in no way restricted to the politics course. Ethics and morals pervade most subjects in Chinese secondary schools in the 1980s.

The content of moral education is a combination of traditional Confucian values, patriotism and socialist principles. Typical manifestations of the moral values implanted through the school system are the regulations and behaviour standards for middle school students and the campaign for the "five things of importance, four things of beauty" (*wu jiang si mei*), which has been the most important ideological education campaign during the period.

New "*Regulations for Middle School Students*" were issued in August 1979 and later slightly revised in 1981.[10] They consist of the following ten points:

1. Love the motherland, love the people, support the Chinese Communist Party, study diligently and prepare to do your utmost for the socialist modernization.

2. Come to school on time, do not be tardy, do not leave early and do not skip classes.

---

9. *RMJY*, no. 7-8 1987, pp. 26-27.

10. Both versions of the regulations can be found in *Zhongguo Jiaoyu Nianjian 1949-1981*, p. 443-444.

3. Listen attentively to the lectures, consider questions carefully, and do your homework earnestly.

4. Keep your body fit and take part in beneficial cultural activities.

5. Take active part in labour and love the fruits of labour.

6. Lead a thrifty and simple life, pay attention to hygiene, do not smoke, do not drink and do not spit on the ground.

7. Observe school discipline, observe public order and abide the laws of the state.

8. Respect the teachers, unite with your fellow students, be polite to others, do not curse others and do not fight.

9. Love the collective, love public property and do not do things harmful to the people.

10. Be honest and modest and correct your mistakes.

These regulations, which hung, framed and behind glass, in a prominent place in every Chinese classroom during the 1980s, combined general and rather abstract principles with down-to-earth rules of behaviour. A list of *"Everyday Behaviour Standards for Middle School Students"*, issued in September, 1988, describes in more detail how middle school students should behave.[11] It consists of forty points divided into five main sections:

The first section is a warning against all the evils that are tempting young people. Boys are not allowed to have long hair, girls should not have their hair curled, use make-up or wear high-heeled shoes. Students are not allowed to use dirty words, to go to commercial dance halls or bars, to gamble, to take part in superstitious activities, to read books about sex or violence, etc.... The eight points of this section can be seen as a form of exorcism against all the "feudal" and "decadent" phenomena which have popped up in the wake of the reforms.

The second section contains rules for proper behaviour, particularly towards fellow students. At the general level students are required to help each other and to respect their teachers. At the more specific level they should stand up when they answer a question from their teacher and ask permission before they enter a fellow student's room.

The third section is about observing discipline in class and in school. Students are here told to take off their caps when the national anthem is played, to come to class on time, to respect the school's property, etc....

---

11. The standards are listed in ZGJYB, Sept. 1., 1988, p. 2.

The fourth section shows that schools are also concerned with students' lives outside the classroom. They should keep their own room in order and wash their own clothes, they should not ask their parents for things which the family cannot afford to buy, they should help and respect their grandparents, etc.... This section has a strong Confucian flavour and even contains the Confucian key virtue of "filial piety" (*xiao*) in its title.

The fifth and last section is concerned with the observation of public law and order, including such rules as traffic regulations and the rules of proper behaviour for sports audiences.

The new standards thus represent a cry for the return of the ideal image of the well-behaved, modest, obedient, well-adapted middle school student of the 1950s. They show no trace of influence from the reform ideas about the need for a more vigorous, independent-minded young generation.

While the regulations and standards mostly consist of restrictions on students' behaviour, the aim of the movement for "five things of importance, four things of beauty" was to establish positive values among the students. The campaign was initiated in February, 1981 as a response to the call of the CCP to establish a "spiritual civilization" matching the "material civilization" created by the four modernizations. This spiritual civilization should guarantee the survival of key communist virtues such as "serving the people, selflessness, strictly observing discipline and self-sacrifice" in an economically developed China, and prevent the "spiritual crisis" which make highly developed capitalist countries "plagued by social decadence, murders, robberies, drugs and suicides".[12]

The "five things of importance" are civilization (material as well as spiritual), good manners, hygiene, order and morals. When students pay attention to these five concepts, they will achieve "the four beauties", i.e. a beautiful spirit, language and behaviour as well as beautiful surroundings.

The content of this campaign, and of moral training in Chinese middle schools in general, can be summed up in a few cardinal virtues: *Selflessness*, *collectivism* and *patriotism*. These virtues all represent the subordination of individual interests to the interests of the group, the family or the nation. This group orientation is a traditional Chinese virtue, which is also stressed in Taiwan in a very different political context.[13] Other central values are *discipline* and *obedience* to the Party, teachers and parents. Obedience is seen as another aspect

---

12. *BR* no. 10, 1981, pp. 18-20.

13. *Wilson 1970*, particularly pp. 19-49.

of selflessness, because the Party represents the interests of the people, the parents represent the interests of the family, etc.... To obey an order from the authorities to go to work in a remote part of China after graduation, for example, thus becomes an act of obedience as well as of service to the people. Finally, *frugality* and *a simple life style* are also seen as important. Students should love manual labour and avoid all the pitfalls of modern society, from fancy clothes to love affairs with classmates.

The *methods* used to implant moral values in the students have not changed much since the 1950s. Stories of *models* are still common. While newspapers have reported on the models of the new age, such as rich peasants and entrepreneurs, these types rarely appear in middle school textbooks. Lei Feng, on the other hand, the model soldier who excelled in self-sacrifice and service to the people, is still held up as a hero to middle school students. This extreme exponent of anti-individualism, who regarded the individual as only a screw in the machine of society, has never lost his appeal to the more conservative part of the leadership.

Rewards are also used to stimulate proper moral behaviour. The title of "three-good-student" (*san hao xuesheng*) is given only to students who show moral-political excellence. As mentioned in Chapter 7, these students are favoured in the university admission procedure, and they also have certain advantages in job allocation. The exact importance of rewards like the "three-good"-title is difficult to estimate, because detailed information about the job allocation system is not available, but they certainly have a considerable influence. Bakken cites one survey of graduates from a specialized middle school, which shows that students who had received honorary titles were nine times more likely to get jobs of the most prestigious category than students who had not received such titles.[14]

If these soft ways of persuasion fail, school authorities can use *sanctions* against students who do not follow the rules. These sanctions can be economical, like in one Hubei school, which decided to fine students 40 *yuan* if they "engage in love affairs which adversely affect their studies" and 15 *yuan* if they "go out together in the evening and do not come home in good time".[15] More important, however, is probably the fact that teachers still see moral training as the very essence of education, so that a student with deviant behaviour will be regarded as a person who has not grasped the essential part of the curriculum and

---

14. *Bakken 1989*, pp 202-203.

15. SWB/FE/0076 B2/1 (16 Feb 1988).

who is therefore unsuited for further advancement up the educational ladder. Although the political screening of students has become less important than in earlier periods, it is my impression from talks with middle school teachers that intellectual merits alone do not qualify a student for an academic career, even under the new meritocratic system. The teachers' evaluation of students' moral qualities also plays a considerable role, and "naughty" students have almost automatically been placed in the slow classes, in the non-key schools, etc.

Moral Education and Social Realities

The values transmitted through moral education have been contradicted not only by the surrounding society, but also more specifically by the hidden curriculum of the schools themselves. Students who really wanted to live up to the publicly sponsored ideals would face enormous difficulties.

Selflessness has been hard to practice inside an extremely competitive educational system. Inside and outside school students have been met with massive propaganda *against* "eating from the same big pot" and other expressions of egalitarianism and *for* more competition (cf. Chapter 3). Inside the classroom, the atmosphere has been extremely competitive and there have been few, if any, incentives to help classmates, because such help would take away time from one's own studies. Concurrently, students have seen the foremost representatives of communist ideals, the Party cadres, being persecuted in large numbers for corruption, official profiteering and other types of selfish behaviour. Other cadres, not subject to persecution, lived in a luxury which could hardly be explained as a result of their service to the people and the nation. Hypocrisy is not a specifically Chinese phenomenon, but the combination of very mixed ideological signals in the media as well as in school (selflessness and competitiveness both being preached at the same time), *and* an obvious lack of moral quality in the leadership have made the well-known "do as I say, not as I do"-trick very difficult to perform convincingly.

The virtues of *obedience* and *discipline* have no doubt been rewarded in the school system, where the teacher-centered method of instruction has put few demands on students' initiative and independent thinking. On the other hand, the universities have cried out for more daring and bold students,[16] and private initia-

---

16. See for example an article by Yang Dongping in *Shijie Jingji Daobao* (World Economic Herald), December 23, 1985, p. 12, translated in *Chinese Law and Government*, vol. 20, no. 2, 1987, pp 9-17. Yang makes the following point (p. 15): "An education system that stresses discipline and following the rules and takes care of everything for the students deprives them of initiative and creativity and reduces them to inertia".

tive and inventiveness have often been propagated in the media. In general, however, keeping discipline is the one part of the moral education curriculum which seems to have been rather successfully implemented. In high quality Chinese middle schools, discipline crises seem rare, and my personal impression is that students are more disciplined than in most other countries. Though high dropout rates and absenteeism indicate discipline problems in less favoured schools, the absence of widespread discussion of disciplinary problems in Chinese educational magazines indicate that it is normally possible for teachers to keep order in the classroom.

The appeals for *a simple life-style* have been counteracted by the sprouting Chinese consumerism, which has followed on the heels of the market-oriented reforms. Advertisements are not as youth-oriented in China as in the West, probably because middle school students do not have much money to spend on consumer goods, but young people have been influenced by the general tendency of "fixing eyes on money" (*xiang qian kan*). Wealth has become a reason for pride rather than for shame, a yardstick for social success which could be displayed without the risk of political stigmatization. Furthermore, films, magazines and TV have introduced Western lifestyle to the young generation on an unprecedented scale, and market mechanisms have encouraged publishing houses to print stories of sex and violence in order to increase their sales, thus adding to the worries of the authorities. During the 1980s, the contours of a youth culture began to appear, representing a life style very different from that of the traditional CCP model cadre, who could wear the same overcoat for twenty years, that is if he did not first give it away to a freezing comrade. Another traditional virtue, the *love of labour*, has likewise been set in a dubious light by social realities. At home, those students aiming at an academic career have been told that they should concentrate on their academic studies instead of doing housework and other manual jobs. In school, they have seen how manual jobs were reserved for academic failures.

The official content of moral education and the general ideological climate of China in the 1980s have thus put varied and even contradictory demands on the middle schools students: they should be selfless but competitive, obedient but independent, frugal but consumer-oriented, and they should respect labour but try to escape it, all at the same time. Again, these contradictions are not unique to China. But because of factors such as the traditional emphasis on moral education, and the abruptness of ideological changes, many students have become extremely confused and have almost totally lost confidence in not only the politics course textbooks, but also in the political system as a whole.

Problems in Students' Ideology

The Chinese leadership has paid close attention to changes in students' ideology since 1980, when they realized that the economic reforms influenced young people's thinking in a number of unpredicted and undesired ways, and they have sponsored many surveys on youth problems. Most of the problems mentioned in these surveys as well as in official and unofficial complaints about the low moral quality of the students of the 1980s can be traced back to the above-mentioned general value conflicts in post-Mao China: Students have been accused of being selfish, being uninterested in politics and in the future of their country, looking down upon manual labour, wasting their time on love affairs and their (and their parents') money on drinking and eating out, etc.... Similar tunes can be heard in almost any country when the old generation is talking about the young one. It is striking, for example, that teachers in Taiwan have the same complaints about their students: they are influenced by individualism, materialism, hedonism, pursuit of profit, the pop culture, etc....[17]

It is characteristic of the Chinese situation, however, that the value clash is felt just as acutely by the well-adapted part of the youth generation. A Shanghai middle school student, for example, published a letter in *Wenhui Bao* in January, 1980, where she described her depression over the gap between ideals and realities:

> Maybe I am prejudiced, but I always feel that the people and phenomena I meet in real life are shrouded in hypocrisy and deception. Many people are selfish. Some people have often made brave statements such as: fight for the four modernizations, fight for communism! Then why do they not want to go to (work in) the villages. Why do they struggle to be employed by a state run enterprise? I accept that the state and the individual cannot be separated, but everyone I meet first thinks for themselves and only then for the state or for other people. This is particularly evident when we look at their attitude towards money. Some middle-aged people are busy all day providing for their own little family, their own children and parents. They feel happy when they can make a good bargain at the market and overjoyed when they can take a sick-leave without a reduction in their bonus.[18]

---

17. *Meyer 1988*, particularly p. 27.

18. *Wenhui Bao*, 20 January, 1980, p. 2.

This letter, and a letter of a very similar content published by *China's Youth* a few months later,[19] generated an overwhelming response from thousands of young people, clearly reflecting the extent of the problem. The girl's teacher could add that she was a model student, a member of the Youth League and an activist in the campaign to learn from Lei Feng.[20] Facing the realities of the 1980s, even such kinds of students found it difficult to remain optimistic about the future of socialist ideals, although they put the blame not on the ideals but on the people who could not live up to them. Other, less Lei Feng-minded, young people found that the collectivist ideals were outdated and incompatible with the modernization ideology.[21]

Considering how much has been written, both in China and abroad, about the young generation's lack of confidence in the Party and in its official ideals,[22] it may be surprising to learn that most surveys show that the large majority of middle school students, when asked about their ideals, their "world outlook", their attitude to official policies, etc... give rather conformist answers.[23] In order to understand this apparent contradiction, one must remember that Chinese survey questions are normally formulated in a way that leaves little doubt about what the correct answer is.[24] Furthermore, students are used to answering moral-political type questions not according to what they think themselves, but according to what they think the teacher will consider to be a correct answer. As one sociological researcher expressed it to Beverley Hooper: "Even when we use anonymous questionnaires, many young people say what they think we want them to say".[25] In this context, giving an "incorrect" answer is paramount to open opposition, and it can be assumed that students giving such answers are only the top of an iceberg of passive discontent. The range of this discontent was forcefully demonstrated during the 1989 student demonstrations.

---

19. This letter was published under the name of Pan Xiao in *ZGQN* no. 5, 1980, pp 3-5.

20. *Wenhui Bao*, 20 January, 1980, p. 2.

21. Some participants in the Pan Xiao debate openly supported individualism, cf. *ZGQN*, no. 8, 1980, pp. 4-6.

22. For a good discussion of youth problems in general in the early 1980s see *Hooper 1985* and *Hooper 1985a*.

23. For a typical example, see the first of the surveys translated in *CE*, vol. 17, no. 4, winter 1984-85.

24. An interesting analysis of this and related problems in Chinese survey research is found in *Rosen 1987a*.

25. *Hooper 1985*, pp. 204-5.

Moral Education and the 1989 Student Demonstrations

Middle school students only played a minor role in the pro-democracy student demonstrations that took place in the spring and summer of 1989. The university students, however, who were the most active force in the movement, were products of secondary education, and even of the most highly esteemed part of it: the key schools. It is therefore natural to comment briefly on the demonstrations in the light of the above discussion of moral education in secondary school.

First of all, the accusation of student apathy towards political and moral questions proved to be false. Students were mobilized in impressive numbers over moral and political issues having little direct connection to their own living standard or other immediate group interests. This is not to say, of course, that such interests did not play a role in creating the general dissatisfaction that led to the demonstrations, but they were never in the focus of attention of either the students or the authorities.

Secondly, the students of the 1980s seemed to have discarded Marxism as an analytical framework. This becomes very clear when we compare their statements with the published materials of the Democracy Movement of 1978-79, which made extensive use of concepts and methods borrowed from Marxism (class analysis, for example) to criticize the absence of democracy in China, the privileges of the cadres, etc.... The 1989 demonstrators produced few theoretical manifestos, and though the events are still too close in time to say for certain, it was my impression from what I overheard of discussions among the students that they were mainly using concepts and rationalizations borrowed from traditional Chinese political culture (for instance in their critique of corrupt cadres) or from the Western democratic tradition.[26] This difference in theoretical basis between the two movements is not surprising when we consider the widely differing experiences of the two generations that took part in them: the Red Guard generation of the first Beijing Spring had seen marxist rhetoric being used to justify the overthrow of high Party and State officials during the Cultural Revolution and they had used it themselves in their struggles with rival factions. The same rhetoric had later been used to suppress the Red Guards, but at least Marxism had proved to be a double-edged sword, which could also be turned against the power-holders. The 1989 student generation had met Marxism only as rigid orthodoxy, as a set of dogmas that should be memorized for the sake

---

26. I was in China from May 13 to June 7, 1989 and talked to a number of student demonstrators in Beijing and Harbin.

of an examination. Marxism had not been used as a framework for a genuine discussion of Chinese society and it had therefore become irrelevant to the students to a degree where "the whole classroom rocks with laughter whenever communism and Marxism-Leninism are mentioned...".[27]

Finally, the demonstrations showed that students did not lack high ideals or the will to sacrifice themselves for the sake of these ideals. The heroism showed by many students during the demonstrations and hunger strikes was similar in nature to the heroism disseminated in textbook stories of Communist heroes. The students' behaviour was not one to be expected from a generation accused of selfishness and hedonism. They showed that they did have lofty ideals, but that these very same ideals almost by definition brought them into conflict with the authorities.

Conclusion

Moral and political education has not disappeared from Chinese secondary education during the reform period. It has survived in the politics course, which is one of the subjects of the university entrance examination, as well as in stories of models and heroes read in other courses, and it has survived via the rules for proper behaviour, the selection of "three-good" students, and the attention which most teachers, true to Chinese traditions, pay to the moral development of their students. Since the beginning of this decade, Chinese leaders have been aware that changes in society would transform students' ideology and morals, and that they would have to intensify moral and political control if they did not want to see the students drift away from traditional communist ideals.

In the politics course and in the moral education carried out in the schools in general, the ideological challenge of the reform period has been met not with an attempt to adapt old principles to the new era, but with a return to the orthodoxy of the pre-Cultural Revolution period. This is different from the adult world, where a relatively open and lively political debate has been going on. Middle school students have been considered too young and immature to take part in a genuine debate of China's future. They have had to wait until a decision would be reached at the top level about the correct interpretation of concepts like socialism and democracy in China today. Because of disagreements inside the leadership and because of the rapid changes in Chinese society such an agreement was never reached. The gap between the ideals preached in school and the social

---

27. This was reported by the Party secretary of a Harbin college to a member of the CCP Politbureau in August 1988, cf. SWB/FE/0232 B2/2-3 (17 Aug 1988).

realities thus became more and more evident to the students, who have responded by losing all interest in the politics course and in official political rhetoric.

In her study of the political socialization of the Red Guard generation, Anita Chan has shown how the gap between real life and the ideals propagated in the schools of the early 1960s eventually led to the desocialization of that generation during the Cultural Revolution:

> The same values and norms once expounded by the authorities would be used by young people....as a yardstick to measure the actual performance of the authorities and the system, and these would be found wanting. The system, the polity, the government and the reified symbols of authority would lose legitimacy.[28]

In the sixties this desocialization was expressed through the extreme violence of the Cultural Revolution. In the 1980s the Party has held much less prestige than it did twenty years before and the expectations of the young generation as to its ideological purity have been more modest. This time it lost its legitimacy not through a "sudden enlightenment" among the students, but through a gradual process of which the crushing of the student demonstrations in June 1989 was only the culmination. This latest loss of legitimacy may be even more serious, because the Party has now lost the support of two successive student generations for its cause.

After the demonstrations the Chinese leaders now again want to strengthen ideological education in, or rather ideological control over, the school system.[29] Ideologically, however, they will have nothing to offer except for the familiar Marxist-Confucian cocktail, which has already proved insufficient. They will therefore have to resort to coercive measures, such as increasing the importance of political criteria in the selection process. Such moves will, however, hardly help to bridge the gap between propaganda and students' experiences in real life.

---

28. *Chan 1985*, p. 190.

29. During the autumn of 1989, this has been a recurrent theme in many statements of top leaders. For one example, see the article by Liu Bin, vice-chairman of the State Education Commission, in *RMJY* no. 10, 1989, pp. 3-4.

10. Social Class, Gender, and Educational Opportunity[1]

The preceeding chapters of this study have dealt with changes in the qualifying and selective functions of secondary education caused by the post-Mao reforms. This final chapter will discuss the effects of the reforms on social distribution, the third and last social function of education to be taken up. In Chapter 6 we saw that the reforms have generally favoured urban over rural areas. We shall now discuss in more detail first the educational opportunities of children from different social classes in post-Mao China, and later the question of girls' education.

Social Class and Educational Opportunities

The relationship between social class and educational opportunities is interesting for several reasons. First of all, the fact that higher education has become the entrance ticket to the Chinese elite means, with certain reservations to which we shall return below, that the recruitment pattern of "key" middle schools will provide information about the social background of this elite which can be useful for understanding its attitudes. Secondly, if the stress on academic qualifications and the absence of class criteria in selection has lead to a marked under-representation of children of workers and peasants in high quality schools, this may, in the long run, turn these groups against the new selection criteria and, perhaps, against other aspects of the educational reforms as well.

Educational inequality in a comparative perspective

The question is interesting in a comparative perspective, too; the connection between socio-economic class and educational opportunities has been intensely debated in the West and in fact can be said to make up a considerable part of an academic discipline: the sociology of education.[2] Surveys have clearly shown that

---

1. An earlier version of this chapter has been published as an article in *The China Quarterly*, cf. *Thøgersen 1987*.

2. For a presentation of the main lines of research in social class and educational inequality see *Karabel and Halsey 1977a*.

schools in Western, capitalist countries favour middle class children over children from working class homes. This bias exists even when children with similar IQ test scores are compared. The reasons for these inequalities are many and complex. Different norms and values shaped by different family surroundings, different "language codes", middle class biases in school norms and in the content of teaching and teaching materials, prejudiced teachers as well as many other factors have all been brought to the light by research.[3]

When we turn to the Soviet Union and Eastern European countries under communist rule, we find a similar picture. Children of privileged groups (intellectuals, white collar employees and cadres) have a much better chance of achieving an education qualifying them for elite status than children of workers and peasants. A high degree of equality was reached in these countries immediately after the communists seized power, but over time the well known pattern of middle class dominance has reappeared.[4]

These international experiences show that we cannot expect China, alone of all countries in the world, to be able to reach a state where equal proportions of all social classes would be recruited in university. As mentioned in Chapter 2, inequalities have existed even in the periods when enrolment criteria have favoured working class children, and given the existing cultural and economic differences between urban and rural areas in China, peasant children will be underrepresented in high quality schools for years to come, no matter which set of selection criteria is used.

However, while the general tendency of social bias in education seems to be universal, the experiences of other countries also show that cultural and social traditions as well as official policies can modify or sharpen educational inequality.[5]

---

3. A number of representative essays on the subject are found in *Halsey 1961* and *Karabel and Halsey 1977*.

4. *Dobson 1977*.

5. Frank Parkin, for example, compares countries ruled by Social Democrats and bourgeois parties respectively, and finds that: "...governments ideologically committed to improving the position of the under-class can bring about certain changes in the overall balance of rewards and opportunities." (*Parkin 1971*, p. 114). Looking at Denmark, E.J. Hansen concludes that "... the post-war objective of providing a larger proportion of working-class children with long-term higher education must be said to have been achieved." (*Hansen 1982*, p. 138). Both authors stress, however, that absolute equality in no way has been achieved.

Chinese Attitudes Towards Educational Inequality
China has a strong tradition for upward social mobility through education, and Chinese history and literature are full of examples of boys of humble origin who climbed to society's top through the examination system. Likewise, the egalitarian Maoist version of communist ideology is deeply embedded in the minds of many Chinese, and the claim that workers and peasants are "masters of the country" in the People's Republic is an important part of CCP ideology. This has placed the CCP under considerable pressure to fight for a more equal representation of workers' and peasants' children in the educational system, and the equal opportunity issue was high on the agenda in earlier periods of the history of the People's Republic (cf. Chapter 2). In spite of this tradition, however, this topic has hardly been publicly discussed at all during the reform decade, and no policy measures have been taken to improve working class children's opportunities in the educational system.

Some Chinese surveys openly admit, almost *a priori*, that children of intellectual families do much better in school than their working class counterparts. In a report on experiments with new teaching methods for character reading for example, it was taken for granted that it was much more difficult to carry out the experiments successfully in one school, where most children were of worker and peasant origin, than in two other schools, where the majority came from intellectual homes.[6] But apparently this has not led to systematic research into the question of how the learning problem of working class children can be overcome. Textbooks in pedagogics and psychology rarely mention social background among the factors which teachers should consider in their tutoring of individual students.

Even when a survey has clearly shown that social background is an important determinant of success in school, the conclusions drawn have often been vague. A survey of forty very successful and forty unsuccessful third and fourth graders in Wuhan is a typical example of this. A psychological test showed that the successful students had better concentration, and were better motivated, more disciplined, etc... than their less successful classmates. At the same time, large differences were found in the social background of the two groups. Half of the successful students came from families where at least one parent had received a higher education against only 3% of the unsuccessful; 86% of the successful students were of intellectual or cadre origin against 33% of the unsuccessful. In the final conclusion, however, these important findings on the social bias of the

---

6. *JYYJ* no. 1, 1979, pp. 89-93.

educational system were not mentioned. Instead the report concluded that success and failure in school is primarily related to psychological factors.[7] As the psychological traits tested actually *define* success in school (discipline, concentration, motivation, etc...) this conclusion cannot be called wrong. But it is characteristic for the tabooing of the problem of social inheritance of educational status that the significant findings on this question had to be underplayed in the conclusion of the survey.

It is not surprising that the authorities have not done anything to encourage research in this field, because the results might throw the new recruitment policy into doubt, be detrimental to the social "rehabilitation" of the intellectuals and focus public attention on existing social inequality and on the privileges of the elite at a time when unity has been a central theme.

Likewise, the researchers themselves lack any personal incentives to discuss the question of educational inequality. When I have brought this issue up in official and private talks with Chinese intellectuals, most of them have expressed the belief that it is only fair that their children achieve success in the educational system. They feel that their children really are better suited for academic studies than children from other classes, because they receive more stimulation in their home environment. Furthermore, they have no other career opportunities, unlike workers' children, who can take over their parents' jobs in industry. Others hold the opinion that unbalanced recruitment really is a problem, but as there is no better alternative to the present selection procedure, it would be better not to make surveys of the question, because the results might stir up popular discontent.

In the absence of Chinese research on the topic, my discussion of social class and educational opportunity will be based mainly on my own survey of six middle schools in Yantai District, Shandong Province.

A Survey of Six Secondary Schools in Yantai
I visited Yantai in April, 1984. Through Beijing Normal University I had requested permission from the Chinese Ministry of Education to carry out a questionnaire survey in that district, because I knew that educational reforms were considered rather successful there and that many basic data on the district had already been published in *Educational Research*.[8] The ministry and the Yantai Educational Bureau accepted my list of 25 questions regarding students' age, sex,

---

7. *JYYJ* no. 12, 1983, pp. 6, 65-69.

8. *JYYJ* no. 11, 1983, pp. 14-24.

Communist Youth League membership, posts held in class (class leader, etc...), preferred academic subjects and future job expectations as well as about their parents' jobs, education, income and Party membership.

Acting on my request to visit general as well as vocational and teachers' training schools, urban as well as rural and key as well as non-key, the bureau drew up a list of seven schools, which I accepted. As I later discovered that one of these schools functioned at post-secondary level, only data from the remaining six have been included here. The schools chosen were probably all in the upper half of their respective categories, but this should not preclude a comparison between them.

Prior to my arrival at the schools I had sent an introduction and a questionnaire ahead of me. On arrival I asked each school to pick out two classes according to varying criteria: grade, specialization (in the vocational schools), etc.... After I had explained to the students the purpose of the survey, they filled in the questionnaires anonymously. Except in the case of one school, either I or my research assistant from Beijing Normal University was present. It is my impression, based largely on the diverse answers to some of the questions, that the students had not been informed about the questions in advance and that they answered them as correctly as they could. Five hundred and eighty-seven students took part in the survey, approximately one hundred from each school.

Problems arose later, however, when I tried to send the questionnaires out of China. The customs authorities would not allow the information on Party and Youth League membership, despite it having been accepted by the Ministry of Education. After about two months, a settlement was reached which unfortunately required that the answers to these two questions be erased.

Yantai District

Yantai District[9] is situated in Shandong Province on the Jiaodong peninsula, and has a population of more than 8 million people. It is a comparatively well-developed area with rich natural resources; 91.5% of the population are registered as "villagers" (nongye hukou), although in the villages themselves more than 55% of the workforce are employed outside of agriculture, in such areas as local industry or commerce.[10] In 1982 the average per capita income in agricul-

---

9. Yantai District (Yantai diqu) is now called Yantai City (Yantai shi). A few of its original counties are now under Qingdao City.

10. JYYJ no. 11, 1983, pp. 20-24.

ture reached 326 *yuan*,[11] well above the national average of 270 *yuan*[12], and in the Chinese press the area has been held up as an example of the success of the agricultural reforms.[13] In 1984 Yantai became one of the fourteen coastal cities open to foreign investors, a move intended to lead to an industrial boom with a subsequent higher demand for qualified manpower.

In the field of education Yantai also compared favourably with most other parts of China. Some key indicators for achievements in this field are listed in Table 10.1. Yantai showed impressive results in popularizing primary and junior secondary education and had a remarkably high (36.5%) transition rate from general senior secondary to tertiary education. I was told that Yantai, though comprising only one tenth of Shandong's population, nevertheless contributed one quarter of all the Shandong students reaching university level. At the National Education Conference held in May, 1985, vice-premier Wan Li praised Yantai for its progress in the field of education, thus giving it a national status which it had not yet achieved at the time of my visit in 1984.[14]

Senior secondary education in Yantai
Developments in senior secondary education in Yantai during the years 1980-84 are shown in Table 10.2. The area followed the national trend of drastically cutting down on general senior middle schools, while to a lesser degree expanding vocational education. The rise in the number of students from 1982 to 1984 can for the most part be explained by the extension of senior secondary school from two to three years in the cities, but it also shows that the decline in enrolment had stopped by this time. In 1984 around 17% of the age cohort in Yantai were enrolled in some kind of senior secondary school, while the corresponding national figure was around 15%.[15] The selection process taking

---

11. Ibid.

12. *Zhongguo Jingji Nianjian* 1983, Sect. III, p. 42.

13. *China Reconstructs* no. 2, 1984, for instance, carried three articles on Yantai which focused on the success of the area.

14. SWB/FE/7968/BII/3.

15. National figure for 1983. Calculations of age cohort are based on the age distribution table (Table 19) in *Census 1982*. All 14- and 15-year-olds, plus 20% of the 16-year-olds (because a certain proportion of schools were already running a three-year program) in 1982 are included. Total number of students from *Statistical Yearbook of China 1984*, p. 488. The Yantai figure has been calculated in the same way, but the total number of students was supplied by Yantai Educational Bureau.

place before senior middle school was thus almost as tough in Yantai as in other places in China.

Shandong Province has been an advanced area as regards the establishing of vocational middle schools. In Yantai District these schools, together with workers' training schools and specialized middle schools, enrolled almost 30% of all students in the spring of 1984, and I was told that the aim was to raise this figure to 35% in the autumn of 1984 and 40% in 1985, which would put Yantai in a favourable position for reaching the national goal of placing 50% of senior middle school students in vocational education before 1990. The structure of vocational education in the district is set out in Table 10.3. Though I was told that vocational schools in particular suffered from a lack of qualified teachers and adequate teaching materials, they already constituted an important alternative to general education and trained people for a wide range of occupations.

Economically as well as educationally, Yantai district was thus above the national average, though it was not as developed as, say, the Beijing or Shanghai regions. Reforms of secondary education had progressed further than in most other areas, but along the same lines. The picture of senior secondary education in Yantai drawn below may thus be more positive than the one found in other localities, but there is no reason to believe that the social effects of the educational reforms or the pattern of social recruitment should differ significantly from that in other places. If anything, there should be less social imbalance in Yantai, because almost all Yantai children were able to graduate from primary school, thereby starting off more equally than children in less developed areas.

The Six Schools Visited
The survey was carried out at the following six institutions:

Yantai No. 2 Middle School in the city of Yantai was considered one of the 19 best middle schools in Shandong[16] and was a provincial level key school. It was founded by American missionaries in 1899 and was a key school even before the Cultural Revolution. It received students from half of Yantai city, which has a population of around 380,000. I shall refer to this school as the "*city key*" school.

Yantai No. 3 Middle School, also in the city, was said to be a non-key general school of average standard. Its senior section accepted students from the whole city of Yantai. Three out of fourteen classes in senior middle school were

---

16. The best key schools of each province are listed in *Zhongguo Jiaoyu Nianjian 1949-1981*, pp. 1096-1103.

vocational, training workers for the textile industry, but none of these were included in the sample. I shall refer to this school as a *"city non-key"* school.

Yantai No. 1 Vocational School, the last city school on the list, was a general middle school until 1981. It had four classes for kindergarten teachers, two classes in art, two in accounting and two in metalwork, all run by the school itself. In addition, there were four classes for fitters, one for brewery workers and one for clock factory workers run in co-operation with the relevant branches of industry. The two classes included in the sample are one for brewery workers and one for accountants. This school is referred to hereafter as a *"city vocational"* school.

Penglai No. 1 Middle School had no junior section, and, in contrast to the other schools visited, its senior section had only a two-year curriculum. Situated in the county town, it recruited students from half of Penglai County (population 479,000), and most of the students were boarders. It was not a provincial level key school, but the county cadres told me that they treated it as a key school at county level, and that it recruited the best of local students. I shall refer to it hereafter as a *"county key"* school.

Laiyang Agricultural Technical School was a general middle school until 1979 when it began to be gradually transformed into an agricultural school. It was run by Laiyang County (population 815,000), and was situated directly outside the county town.The students, who were recruited from among junior secondary school graduates from the whole county, were all boarders. The school offered two specialities: fruit-growing and grain-farming. I shall refer to this school as an *"agricultural"* school.

Laiyang Teachers' Training School was run directly by Yantai District and trained primary school teachers for village schools. Students were recruited from among junior middle school graduates of five counties in the district and they all returned to their home county after graduation. The history of this school goes back to 1938, when it was established by the CCP in its Shandong base area. I shall refer to it as a *"teachers' training"* school.

The last three schools on the list will be grouped together as *"rural"* schools, as they recruited students from mainly agricultural areas, while the first three schools will be labeled as *"urban"* schools. The city key, city non-key and county key schools are referred to collectively as *"general"* schools; the remaining three are all *"vocational"* schools.

Basic conditions. The schools were all of a reasonable standard with regard to buildings and equipment, though the three urban schools, not surprisingly, were in better condition than the rural schools. The city key school seemed to have the best equipment and the most pleasant surroundings. Whether it also had more money to spend per student is hard to say, as the answers from the six schools concerning finances unfortunately turned out to have no common denominator.

Table 10.4 shows that neither urban schools nor key schools had the advantage of fewer students per class or lower student/teacher ratios. On the contrary, it seems that the higher prestige of the key schools forced them to accept more students into each class. The average student/teacher ratio for China's middle schools was 17.2 in 1984,[17] so Yantai is in this respect close to the average standard.

The teachers. As shown in Table 10.5, the formal level of the teachers' education varied among the six schools, but the standard was reasonably high in all of them. The number of university graduates at the teachers' training school was surprisingly high, but this can be explained by the fact that this school was run directly by Yantai District and thus received a bigger share of the candidates assigned to work in the district than schools run by the lower levels. Among the remaining schools, the two key schools had better formally qualified teachers than the rest, but this may well have been the case even before the introduction of the key school system. In any case, the differences were not as extreme as might have been expected from the key school debate in the media.

Career prospects. In contrast to other Chinese cities at that time, I was told that Yantai in 1983 was able to offer jobs or further education to all students who passed the junior or senior middle school final examinations. The distribution of 1983 senior middle school graduates from the six schools by job and education can be seen in Table 10.6. It is quite evident that the future careers of students were to a very large extent determined by the calibre of the secondary school attended.

The two key schools both offered their students a fair opportunity for entering university. A quite large proportion of key school students, however, were placed under "other or no occupation", which in most cases meant that they were preparing themselves to retake the university entrance examination, having failed the first time. A key school education was thus no guarantee of a university place.

It is quite surprising that the highest transition rate to university or other further education was found in the county key school (61%) and not, as might be expected, in the prestigious city key school (40%). The Yantai Educational

---

17. *Statistical Yearbook of China 1985*, p. 585.

Bureau maintained that this was not a unique case. The county key schools generally had the highest transition rates in the district, some of them as high as 80%, which contrasts with information from other areas, where county key schools find it very hard to compete with urban schools. One reason for the unusual figures may be that primary and junior secondary education is comparatively well developed in the villages of Yantai District. Another factor may be that the county key schools have a larger recruiting base than the city schools.

In the remaining schools the students were for the most part the future skilled workers and medium-level technicians. Though all city vocational school graduates are designated as "workers", it should be remembered that this school trains people for blue- as well as white-collar professions. Future agricultural technicians, agricultural school teachers and peasants in specialized branches of agricultural production (*zhuanye hu*) were found in the agricultural school, and trainee village primary school teachers in the teachers' training school. Graduates from vocational schools seem to have all found jobs appropriate to their education, but the price they paid for this security is that they lost practically all chance of going to university.

The future careers of the city non-key school students will in general differ from the pattern found in 1983. The 1983 graduates from this school all came from vocational classes, since general senior secondary school was in the process of being extended from two to three years. I expect the career pattern of students from this school to come to resemble that of the city key school, except that probably fewer students will go to university.

Thus, there is a close relation between the type of middle school attended and occupation after graduation. This means that the data on social recruitment into different types of secondary schools also provide some information about the question of social recruitment to different occupations.

Political organizations. The most important political organization recruiting Chinese middle school students is the Communist Youth League, which is, among other things, a preparation for later Party membership. It is interesting to note that the Youth League had relatively more members in the city key school (32% of all students including junior middle school) than in the other urban schools (12% at both schools). The same pattern was found among rural schools, which, however, had no junior section and therefore a higher proportion of Youth League members. The county key school and the teachers' training school had relatively more League members (66% and 73% respectively) than the agricultural school (40%). Thus the Youth League evidently recruits more members from among future intellectuals than from among future workers and peasants.[18]

Yantai's Line in Educational Reforms

The orientation of education in Yantai appeared to be less elitist than in most other places in China. The concentration of qualified teachers in key schools was moderate, and the transition rate from the finest key school in the district to university was only slightly above average. I was also told that the streaming of students into "fast" and "slow" classes still common in other areas at this time had been stopped in Yantai.

The moderate key school strategy followed in Yantai has been described in a report from the educational authorities in Rongcheng County, which is part of Yantai District. In this county each key school was only allowed to enroll a certain number of the most gifted students, while the rest were recruited from within the local school district. At the same time the key schools were made responsible for the progress of a number of non-key schools to whom they were to send some of their experienced teachers. According to the report, the Rongcheng key schools enrolled as many as 53% of all secondary school students, thereby clearly modifying the "key" concept. In spite of this, the non-key schools, with only 47% of the students, contributed 30% of all Rongcheng students entering university.[19] This indicates considerably less inequality between key and non-key schools and more emphasis on the model role of key schools than in other areas.

If it is true that an elitist school system creates greater social bias in recruitment, then the imbalances found in Yantai may well be smaller than in other parts of China, where a more rigorous version of the key school strategy has been practiced.

Students' Social Background

A detailed picture of the social recruitment pattern to the six schools emerged from the Yantai students' answers to five questions concerning their parents' occupation, education and income. As urban and rural schools recruit students from very different social backgrounds, the two groups of schools will be treated separately.

---

18. The figures for Yantai were given to me at interviews with the principals of the six schools.

19. *Shandong Jiaoyu (Shandong Education)* no. 11, 1983, pp. 6-7.

Urban schools. In the urban schools, the social background[20] of general school students clearly differed from that found at the vocational school (Table 10.7). There were fewer children of manual workers in the general schools, 20% against 37% in the vocational school, and more children of cadres. Correspondingly, the educational level of the fathers of general school students (Table 10.8) was somewhat higher than those of the vocational school students, where 24% of the fathers had at most primary education compared to 14% at the key and 18% at the non-key general school. The income level of the parents of key school students, on the other hand, was lower than that at the other schools (Table 10.9). This is also true for single occupational categories (cadres, intellectuals and workers). This is rather surprising when compared to other countries, and though part of the reason may be that the students found it difficult to answer this question correctly, I also believe that it indicates that money is not a particularly important factor in deciding urban students' educational careers. At the vocational school there was no significant difference between future brewery workers and accountants in regard to their parents' jobs, income and education.

Comparing students' fathers with the occupational and educational profile of the male city workforce, aged 35-39 (Tables 10.7 and 10.8), there was an evident over-representation of fathers with tertiary or secondary education. Half of the fathers of city key school students, for instance, had received at least senior secondary education, while this was the case for only around one quarter of the total non-peasant workforce in this age group. Even taking into account Yantai's proud traditions in the educational field, it seems safe to conclude that children of manual workers and children of parents with less than secondary education are to a large degree screened out before reaching senior secondary school, and that they, if they get this far, are more likely than others to end up in the vocational stream. The big winners in the admission game are the children

---

20. The classification of parents' occupations is based on answers to three questions. Students were asked (1) to place their parents in one of six categories: workers, peasants, employees, cadres, professionals and soldiers; (2) to place their parents according to the economic sector in which they worked (industry, agriculture, etc...); and (3) to describe their parents' actual work function. In the final classification the answers to all three questions were used to place the parents in one of the following groups: *cadres* - people with leadership or administrative functions in state and party organs or enterprises, including military personnel; *intellectuals* - people engaged in mental work who have received at least specialized secondary education and school teachers without regard to their education background; *non-manual workers* - people in the commerce and service sectors without leadership functions, including accountants, shop assistants, office staff, nurses, postmen and laboratory workers; *manual workers* - workers in industry, construction and transport and urban artisans; *peasants* - peasants, fishermen, village craftsmen and a few basic-level agricultural technicians.

of cadres, and to a lesser degree intellectuals, who between them held 60% of the seats in the two general middle schools.

Another interesting feature is that the real dividing line as far as family background was concerned seemed to exist between general and vocational schools rather than between key and non-key students. This indicates, I believe, that the difference in opportunities for the children of workers and cadres is here to stay, because while the key school system has been under revision, the division between general and vocational schools is an important and permanent part of the reforms.

Rural schools. Among the rural schools, the key school and the teachers' training school showed much the same recruitment pattern (Table 10.10). Half of the children came from peasant families, while just more than a quarter were of cadre or intellectual origins. At the agricultural school there was a much larger proportion of peasant students (77%).[21] When comparing this with the male countryside workforce of similar age, it was evident that recruitment to the agricultural school corresponded very closely to the general occupational pattern, while peasants were under-represented at the two schools preparing students for non-manual jobs.

The figures for fathers' education (Table 10.11), however, show that the countryside youth recruited to the agricultural school were not even an average group. Only around one quarter of the fathers of students in all three schools had received no education above primary school level, while this was the case for almost three quarters of the male Shandong population of comparable age. A further breakdown of the figures shows that of the 66 peasants sending their children to the agricultural school, two thirds had received at least junior secondary education. It can thus be concluded that parents' educational level is an important factor in deciding the educational prospects of rural children, and

---

21. At the teachers' training and agricultural schools, I was told by the principals that 98% and 100% of the students respectively were of peasant origin. What was probably meant was that all students possessed a countryside registration (*nongye hukou*) inherited from their mothers. If the few statistics on social recruitment to higher education released to foreign scholars (see in particular *Pepper 1984*, pp. 135-40) have been calculated using the same method, they substantially overestimate the number of genuine peasant students. In the Yantai survey only students who put their father's job in the category of "peasant" *and* answered that the father was actually doing agricultural labour have been included in the "peasant" category. In this way I hope to have screened out some (but not necessarily all) of the village cadres and workers in rural industry.

that this is the case not only for the traditional general schools, but also for the new agricultural schools.

The survey leaves little doubt that social inequality in access to senior secondary education exists in post-Mao China. At the same time, however, the figures clearly show that access to even the best senior middle schools is in no way restricted to children of cadres and intellectuals. In both general urban schools, 37% of the children came from working-class homes, and in the county key school, which sent as many as 61% of its students on to tertiary education, half of the students had peasant fathers. This means that avenues of upward social mobility for the offspring of workers and peasants do exist, at least in relatively well-off areas such as Yantai, and this may well serve to put a damper on protests against the social bias of the new middle school system.

Social background and school performance
Does parents' occupational and educational status also influence students' school performance once the students have passed the hurdle and gained access to senior secondary school? This question is of great importance as a senior middle school diploma, even from a key school, is no guarantee of admission to university or finding a job. Good marks in senior middle school foreshadow success at the university entrance examination and therefore might indicate a promising career.

I had expected a correlation to exist between parents' education and students' academic performance, as parents with a higher education are better able to tutor their children and stimulate their intellectual interests, but no such correlation was found in the Yantai sample. Table 10.12 shows the aggregate marks in Chinese, mathematics, physics, English and politics for students from the three general schools classified according to their fathers' education. An almost equal proportion of each group passed the 400 points' mark, while there were relatively fewer students from homes with little education among the students scoring 360 points or less. When, however, the individual schools, classrooms or subjects were analyzed, no consistent picture emerged, and the only conclusion to be drawn seems to be that parents' education had no independent influence on the academic performance of senior middle school students.

The occupational status of parents, on the other hand, did exert a certain influence on school performance, but not in the sense that children from high-status homes got better marks than others. Table 10.13 shows that children of cadres scored less than other students in general schools, and this pattern was found for each of the five school subjects on the list. In the city vocational school, on the other hand, the children of cadres were average achievers. Their performance thus seems to be below average in schools where they are over-represented, indicating that some of them had been pushed further ahead in the education system than their abilities justified.

The children of intellectuals performed markedly better than other students only at the city key school, where 85% scored 400 points or more in the five selected subjects, against only around 60% of other social groups, while they did not excel above the mean in the other schools. The children of peasants scored just as well or even better than their classmates, and nor did the children of workers seem to be academically inferior to other students.

While children from low-status families thus have difficulty gaining access to senior secondary schools, their academic performance - once they are admitted - is not adversely affected by their social background. This phenomenon is evidenced in other countries as well, at least at college level. If the word "college"' was replaced by "senior middle school", the following conclusion to a survey of American college students could also apply to Chinese middle school students:

> The student who gets into college has already overcome whatever handicaps his home environment offered; once there, his chances of graduating are much more dependent upon his ability and much less upon his family background than were his chances of getting into college in the first place.[22]

Not only school performance but also career plans were more or less the same for all social groups (Table 10.14). When asked what they wanted to do after graduation, the overwhelming majority of general school students from all social groups answered that they wanted to continue into some kind of tertiary education. In the vocational schools a corresponding majority declared that they wanted to take up the trade in which they were being trained. Almost one quarter of the city vocational school students had ambitions to continue their education, but these students were spread equally between all social groups. The only marked difference in student ambition was that children from intellectual families were less interested than other groups in joining the army.

In each middle school class, one student was appointed class leader, while others were responsible for spare-time activities or for one of the school subjects.

---

22. Dale Wolfle, *America's Resources of Specialized Talent* (New York, 1954), p. 163. Quoted here from *Karabel and Halsey 1977*, p. 198.

In the classrooms surveyed each social group had a share of these posts corresponding fairly closely to its proportion of the student body.

All these facts point in the same direction: the social bias in recruitment to university, which was recognized by the Chinese authorities as early as 1978,[23] and which has been further documented by more recent information[24] is primarily a reflection of a pattern existing at least as early as the senior middle school level. Moreover, the streaming of students taking place after junior middle school is likely to be much more important than university entrance examinations for screening out students from working-class homes.

Social factors, however, may well also influence the selection taking place between senior middle school and university, in spite of the fact that working-class children have good academic records in senior middle school. As shown below, an underprivileged group who does very well in senior middle school might still prove unsuccessful in their attempt at university admission. This seems to be the case, at least, for girls.

Boys and Girls in Senior Secondary School
While information about students' family background is rather scarce, statistics on the sex ratio in Chinese schools have been published regularly. Table 6.4 showed that the ratio of female students in higher education went up from around one fourth to one third during the Cultural Revolution decade. It fell back to less that one fourth after the introduction of the university entrance examination in 1977, but has risen slowly to one third again over the last ten years. In middle school, the girls have maintained around 40% of the places, a level which they reached in 1976. Also in primary education the girls have held a stable share of the places since 1976, around 45%.

Despite such statistics being available, the underrepresentation of girls in secondary and tertiary education attracts relatively little attention in the debate over educational issues in China today. The question of female school dropouts has been taken up but is seen mainly as a question of parents' traditional

---

23. In the discussions following the 1978 university entrance examinations a Ministry of Education spokesman admitted: "There are a greater number of college students from intellectual families than from workers' and peasants' families because the former have better conditions and environment for learning." He did not see this as a problem, however; *BR* no. 30, 1978, p. 18.

24. See, for example, the figures for the family background of undergraduates enrolled at Hangzhou University (1983-86) and Beijing University (1982-85) in *CE*, vol. 21, no. 4, winter 1988-89, pp. 25 and 53. Data for a few other universities around 1980 are given in *Pepper 1984*, see particularly pp. 107-116 and 135-41.

ideology, not as a problem that could be tackled in school. No reference is made to the problem of female underrepresentation in textbooks on education used at teachers' training schools, and it is rarely mentioned in educational magazines.

Exceptions can, of course, be found. One interesting survey carried out by teachers in a girls' middle school in Shanghai tried to trace the reasons for female underachievement and found that girls are disadvantaged mainly because they have fewer social contacts and participate less in extracurricular activities.[25] This indicates that social and cultural rather than biological factors are the main reasons for female underrepresentation. This a hypothesis that is strongly supported by the Yantai data.

Table 10.15 shows that girls and boys were equally represented in the urban general schools, while girls made up only one third of the agricultural and teachers' training school students. In the county key school, 43% of the students were girls - more than in other rural schools, but less than in the city. The picture of equality in enrolment in city schools was supported by visits to Beijing schools, where around half of the students, even in the most prestigious schools, were girls. The problem of underrepresentation of girls in senior middle school thus seems to be restricted to the countryside.

At the vocational school, there existed typical variations in the distribution of boys and girls in the different specializations (Table 10.16). There was a female majority among future non-manual workers and workers in light industry, while males outnumbered females in classes for metal workers. This corresponds to the existing distribution of men and women in the labour force, where men dominate heavy industry, while women primarily work in light industry and the service sector.[26] It is worth noting, however, the large proportion of girls among future accountants, artists and engine fitters, all jobs carrying relatively high social prestige.

Social differences in the attitude to girls' education can be seen from Table 10.17. It must be noted here that the main reason girls are overrepresented in the sample is due to the large number of girls in the two classes surveyed at the vocational school. Bearing this in mind, it can be seen that not only peasants but also workers and intellectuals living in rural areas send more boys than girls to senior secondary school. It seems that a traditional adverse attitude towards

---

25. Shisan Nü Zhong (No. 13 Girls' Middle School), "Yanjiu nüzhong jiaoyu de tedian" ('Research on the Characteristics of Education in a Girls' Middle School'), *Shanghai shi 1983*, pp. 22-34.

26. *Census 1982*, pp. 344-349.

female education influences workers and intellectuals in rural areas just as heavily as it does the peasants. The intellectuals concerned are for a large part village school teachers, and the majority of the workers are probably employed in small collective enterprises in the countryside. Only the cadres seem to be immune to rural influence. It is possible, of course, that the many years of political agitation for sexual equality during the Cultural Revolution have influenced this group more than the others, but a more likely explanation is that they are simply able to send almost all their children, not just the boys, to middle school.

In the urban schools there was a remarkably large majority of girls among working-class students. One explanation could be that more working-class boys than girls go to workers' training schools or inherit their fathers' jobs in industry through the replacement system.

The survey further showed that it is not lack of ambition that keeps girls out of university.[27] In all categories of schools more girls than boys expressed a wish to go on to higher education. Their interests, however, differed from those of the boys. Asked which three subjects they liked the best and which the least, the Yantai students followed the pattern found in Chinese surveys:[28] boys preferred science subjects, while girls were more attracted to Chinese and English. In the general schools, for instance, 51% of the boys against 26% of the girls mentioned physics as one of their favourite subjects, while in the case of English the opposite was true: 22% of the boys and 57% of the girls put the subject in their top three. This tendency is evident worldwide[29] and reflects patterns already established through primary socialization in the family; it works to the particular disadvantage of girls in China, where the university structure is dominated by natural sciences and engineering.[30]

It is a popular notion in China that "girls in primary and junior middle school show better performance and get better results than boys, but when they get to senior middle school they gradually fall behind the boys",[31] and this is claimed as the main reason for female underrepresentation at tertiary level

---

27. This finding is supported by Zhang Yiqing's survey in *Ye 1985*, pp. 158-182, particularly p. 171.

28. See for example the survey by Luo Yicun and Shen Jiaxian in *JYYJ* no. 8, 1983, pp 58-63 (translation in *CE*, vol. 17, no. 4, winter 1984-85, pp. 41-61).

29. See *Kelly 1981* and *GASAT 1983*.

30. Only 6% of the students admitted to institutions of higher learning in 1987 were enrolled in liberal arts as compared to 33% in engineering. *Zhongguo Tongji Nianjian 1988*, p. 881.

31. *JYYJ* no. 12, 1981, pp. 43-45 (p. 43).

schools.[32] This claim is substantiated by some Chinese surveys which show that the third year of junior middle school is the time where boys surpass girls academically, at least in the science subjects.[33] It is, however, contradicted by others,[34] and it certainly did not hold true in the six Yantai schools.

In the three general schools, there was not much difference between the achievements of boys and girls in mathematics, physics and politics, but in the girls' favourite subjects, Chinese and particularly English, they got much higher marks than the boys. The result was that the girls' total scores in these five subjects, which were all important at the university entrance examinations, were considerably higher than that of the boys (Table 10.18). Fifty-six per cent of the girls scored 400 points or more against 33% of the boys. Among those scoring only 360 points or less, we find 34% of the boys but only 15% of the girls.

The three vocational schools did not teach all the five subjects mentioned, but if we concentrate on the three subjects taught in all schools, namely Chinese, mathematics and politics, a picture very similar to that of the general schools is revealed. It is, in fact, impossible to find any school subject in any group of schools where boys scored substantially higher than girls.

The Yantai data thus throw doubt on the presumption that girls fall behind boys academically in senior middle school and that this should be the main reason why so few of them are admitted to university. It shows, on the contrary, that girls in Yantai schools held an equal share of the places in the schools providing their students with the best chances for continuing on to university, that they were ambitious and that they got better marks than the boys. The reasons for female underrepresentation at the level of tertiary education should probably be found elsewhere. One reason is undoubtedly that they prefer humanistic subjects, which have low priority in China. Another reason is that universities (and other schools as well) often directly discriminate against girls by demanding a higher entrance exam score from them than from the boys.[35] But the main factor is probably the traditional negative attitude towards girls' education in China. The

---

32. *GMRB*, 28 February 1986, p. 3.

33. This is the result reached, for example, in a survey conducted by Liu Suyun, cf. *Ye 1985*, pp. 203-237.

34. See for example Zhang Yiqing's survey presented in *Ye 1985*, pp. 158-182.

35. That some universities and even middle schools demand higher passing rates from girls is mentioned in *JYYJ* no. 6, 1983, pp. 50-57, particularly pp. 55-56. Other articles discussing the problem of discrimination against girls in education and employment can be found in *CE*, vol. 22, no. 2, summer 1989.

fact that girls are more competitive in urban areas than in the more tradition-bound countryside supports this conclusion.

If we return to the question of social class and educational opportunity, similar obstacles may well face children from families of low social status, though they too perform well academically in senior middle school. It may well be, for instance, that children from high-status homes are more persistent in their attempts to pass the university entrance examinations.[36] It is also possible that students of worker and peasant origin are more likely to apply to low-status institutions. This last hypothesis was supported by a visit to a specialized middle school in Beijing, where I was told by the principal that the clientele had changed in recent years. Before 1978 the school enrolled many children of intellectuals and high-level cadres. These students, the principal said, now tried to gain access to university instead, while the specialized midlde schools were being taken over by children of workers and lower-level cadres.[37] Similarly, a specialized middle school in Yantai training technicians for the fishing industry enrolled almost exclusively students of peasant origin.[38] A top-quality key school in Beijing, on the other hand, where 80% of the students came from intellectual or cadre families, informed me that the large majority of their graduates were recruited by key universities.[39] In spite of the good academic performance of under-privileged groups in senior middle school a new social selection may therefore be taking place between senior middle school and university, increasing the social imbalance in recruitment.

This hypothesis is contradicted, however, by the data on student recruitment from Hangzhou University and Beijing University. According to these data, only 45% of the students enrolled at Beijing University and 30% of those at Hangzhou University in 1985 were of cadre or intellectual origin.[40] If we compare this to

---

36. Among American college dropouts (a group resembling the Chinese students who fail to pass the university entrance examinations) social class is an important determinant of who will transfer or return to college later in their career. Bruce K. Eckland "Social class and college graduation: some misconceptions corrected". *American Journal of Sociology*, no. 70, July 1964, pp. 36-50, quoted in *Karabel and Halsey 1977*, p. 197.

37. This school was the Beijing School of Electricity (*Beijing Dianli Xuexiao*).

38. This school was the Shandong Province School of Fishery and Aquaculture (*Shandong Sheng Shuichan Xuexiao*). A sample survey of 71 students at this school showed that they were "genuine" peasant students, not just registered in a village.

39. This school was Beijing Normal University's No. 2 Attached Middle School.

40. *CE*, vol. 21, no. 4, winter 1988-89, pp. 25 and 53.

Yantai, where 61% of the students in the city key and 36% of those in the county key came from the same groups, it seems that those children of workers and peasants, who graduate from a key middle school have already overcome their social "handicap". Much more complete data are needed, however, before we can draw conclusions on this question.

Conclusion

Middle school reforms in Yantai had, as far as I could ascertain, been a success. The social imbalance in Yantai's middle school system was thus not a result of an imperfect implementation of the reforms, but a problem inherent in the new structure.

The survey shows that the problem of unequal representation of different social groups was strongest in general middle schools, but also existed in vocational schools. There were a disproportionate number of children whose parents had received a tertiary or secondary education in all the schools. In the academically inclined general schools children of cadres were strongly overrepresented. On the other hand, it also shows that at least in well-off areas like Yantai there were possibilities for upward social mobility through the educational system and that children of workers and peasants, though underrepresented, were in no way excluded from the best middle schools.

The girls had great academic success in the Yantai schools and were just as ambitious as the boys. This indicates that factors other than academic results lie behind their underrepresentation at the university level.

The survey confirms the impression, common among ordinary Chinese, that the leadership stratum is mainly recruiting its successors from its own offspring. This tendency is probably reinforced in the selection taking place in the job allocation process after graduation from university, where children of cadres can make use of their family connections to get the best posts. We already know that female candidates are being discriminated against in this process.[41]

Will the social imbalance in recruitment discredit educational reforms in the eyes of the public? Not necessarily. In the first place, we do not know whether things were much different during the preceding decade. Workers and peasants may well feel that their children's chances for upward social mobility are not much smaller than they have always been, particularly because the number of white collar jobs is increasing as an effect of the economic modernization. Secondly, the absence of precise data and public debate on the question

---

41. See for example *CE*, vol. 22, no. 2, summer 1989, pp. 9-13.

in China may keep it out of the limelight for some time. On the other hand, we saw during the Cultural Revolution how social imbalance in recruitment to the educational system can suddenly become an extremely disruptive issue.

In a comparative perspective we can see that China has not come any farther than other countries in solving the question of social imbalance in education. What is more, very little research is being carried out to identify the problems of social imbalance and gender bias in Chinese middle schools and universities, and virtually nothing is being done to overcome them.

11. Conclusion

The arrest of the "Gang of Four" in October, 1976 and the brutal crushing of the pro-democracy demonstrations in June, 1989 marked respectively the beginning and the end, at least temporarily, of a period of fundamental educational reforms in China, not least so in the field of secondary education. During these more than twelve years, the contents of all the major social functions of education analyzed in this study have been radically changed.

The quality of the *qualifications* transmitted in secondary education are difficult to measure in any exact way, but there are some general trends which stand out quite clearly. In quantitative terms we have seen a decrease in the share of the age cohort enrolled into junior and senior secondary school as well as the persistent existence of a serious dropout problem. The *technical qualifications* of those who have completed secondary education have become less uniform in content as well as in standard and are now more institution-dependent following the increasing diversification of secondary education into different types of schools (urban/rural, key/non-key, general/vocational).

As for the *general skills,* there is little doubt that the level of formal academic competence in, for example, mathematics and Chinese has been raised among the students of the more privileged middle schools. The qualifications of the teaching force have been improved, and the total devotion with which many students and teachers have studied and taught over the last ten years has been impressive. Other students, however, particularly those in rural areas, but also the majority of urban students who have been unable to enter university, have benefitted little from this rise in academic standards. This is due in part to the fact that the education of these students has often been ignored and that most schools have neglected to teach about the practical application of the facts and formulas memorized for the sake of the examinations.

Strengthening the teaching of *specific skills* has been one of the major purposes of the reforms, and the vocationalization of senior middle school has been an important achievement in the 1980s. But in spite of its expansion, the vocational education system still only reaches less than 10% of the age cohort and does therefore far from make up for the negligence of applied knowledge and skills in general schools. China's modernization drive needs all the skilled workers and middle level technicians that vocational middle schools can train, but it also requires a high practical skill level among peasants and common workers, and this is where the middle school system of the 1980s has failed.

In September, 1983, Deng Xiaoping created a motto for one of Beijing's elite schools: "Education must turn it's face towards modernization, towards the world and towards the future".[1] These "three towards" (*san ge mianxiang*) have been officially canonized as "the general principle of the educational reforms" and are said to "point out the strategic direction of educational work in the new era".[2] But as the educational system turned its face in these directions it simultaneously turned its back to the problems of the backward sectors and regions of the country, to those students who for some reason were unable to live up to the new standards and to those experiences of the past which had demonstrated the need for secondary education to do more than just transmit academic qualifications to the minority of the population who will work in the modern sectors of the economy. The modernization of agriculture, for example, one of the "four modernizations", has not been stimulated by educational reforms. An analysis of the skill requirements in rural areas would have pointed towards very different solutions to the problems confronting rural schools after the Cultural Revolution decade. Most of the participants in the on-going discussion on how to make rural education fit the needs of the villages openly admit this and recommend adding more courses related to agriculture and adapted to local conditions to rural schools. After ten years of competition in a game where the cities set the rules, rural schools now appear to be turning to a model better suited to rural needs. The detour around academic and highly selective schools appears to have been conditioned by such factors as the political leaders' vision of a modern, economically developed China with an educational system fully up to the standards of the industrialized world and the ambitions of the rural population of upward social mobility through the educational system rather than by the actual needs of the villages.

Turning to the status of the *ideological qualifications*, the Chinese top leaders have openly admitted the failure of their attempt to curb the ideological influence of liberal economic reforms on the Chinese youth through moral education. In March, 1989, Deng Xiaoping told a foreign visitor that education was the field where China had made the most serious mistakes over the past ten years, and he later added that he mainly had been thinking of moral and political

1. *Jiaoyu Gaige*, p. 287.
2. *Jiaoyu Cidian*, p. 21-22.

education.[3] The leaders, particularly the orthodox ones, hoped that moral education could work as a cure for the ideological and social "ills" which the economic reforms brought in their wake. It was to be a filter that would prevent the decadence and political liberalism of the Western world from creeping into the young minds while letting through its dynamic and enterprising spirit. However, the gap between ideological propaganda and social realities was too wide, and the students were left deeply frustrated and disenchanted.

The *selective function* of secondary schools has been extremely important for the outcome of the reforms in secondary education. The examination system succeeded in mobilizing previously unexplored resources by increasing students' motivation for study. But the increased competition, one of the key concepts in the reform ideology, has also had its price. When the examination system was reintroduced, students, parents, teachers and officials all tried to maximize their profit from the new intellectual market mechanism. All intellectual and material resources were invested where the highest short-term profits could be made, namely in the education of the future elite, while the "basic construction work" among the majority of the students was ignored. The narrow restrictions on admission to university, the importance of formal education for social prestige and career opportunities, the danger of alternative selection criteria being abused by the powerful strata of society, as well as the Chinese tradition for gearing education to the needs of the examination system made futile all countermeasures against the problems created by the new selection methods.

In the perspective of *social distribution,* the educational reforms have favoured the urban population and led to a larger degree of inequality in access to education between children from different social classes. For the intellectuals the economic reforms have had very limited benefits, but the reforms in education have served to partly compensate them for the rise in income that other groups have experienced. Children from intellectual families often come off best in the examinations, and the academic selection criteria have strengthened the position of the teachers inside and outside the classrooms. But most importantly, the introduction of academic competence as the main criteria for selection inside the educational system has strengthened the intellectuals' self-respect; it symbolizes the official recognition of their vital role in China's modernization. The promise that intellectual ability and educational achievements rather than political influence or class background should become the entrance card to the Chinese elite has probably been just as crucial for the intellectuals' support of the

---

3. *BR* no. 28, (July 10-16), 1989, pp. 14-17.

post-Mao leaders as the de-collectivization of agriculture was for parts of the rural population. In this way educational reforms have been part of the larger redistribution process in post-Mao China.

If the radical reformers had gained the upper hand in the summer of 1989 so that economic and political reforms had been allowed to continue, new challenges would soon have faced the educational system. A market-oriented economy would have increased the number of attractive career opportunities for talented young people without college diplomas, thereby taking some of the pressure off the examination system. Likewise, a successful labour market reform could have changed the employment pattern in a way that would make vocational and technical educations more attractive. Changes in these directions were perceptible in the latter half of the 1980s, and they might in the long run have proved to be a better cure for the "diploma disease" than all the rules and regulations issued by the State Education Commission, and might even have made it difficult for the universities to attract enough qualified students.

However, the radical reformers lost the battle for power and the present political situation makes a discussion of the future prospects for Chinese secondary education seem rather pointless at the moment. The orthodox leaders will use all their energy to cling to power and their educational policies will thus necessarily serve this aim. They will try to strengthen the ideological control over the content of education and over the students, but it seems unlikely that they will be able to introduce any major new structural reforms. When the dust settles and the present power struggle is over, the victors will probably carry out a re-evaluation of the reform strategy and of the results of the first twelve years of reforms after the death of Mao Zedong. At that time, new educational policies may well again become the first signal of which way the wind is blowing.

Abbreviations

BR	*Beijing Review*
CE	*Chinese Education*. A Journal of Translations. M.E. Sharpe, New York.
GMRB	*Guangming Ribao* (Guangming Daily)
JYYJ	*Jiaoyu Yanjiu* (Educational Research)
RMJY	*Renmin Jiaoyu* (People's Education)
RMRB	*Renmin Ribao* (People's Daily)
SWB/FE	*Summary of World Broadcasts, Part 3, Far East*, BBC Monitoring, Reading
ZGQN	*Zhongguo Qingnian* (China's Youth)
ZGJYB	*Zhongguo Jiaoyu Bao* (Chinese Education News)
ZXXJY	*Zhong-xiaoxue Jiaoyu* (Secondary and Primary Education), Baokan ziliao xuanhui (Selections from newspapers and magazines), Zhongguo Renmin Daxue shubao ziliao zhongxin, Beijing.

Bibliography

Achievement of Education:
> Department of Planning, Ministry of Education: *Achievement of Education in China. Statistics 1949-1983*, Renmin Jiaoyu Chubanshe, Beijing, 1984. (In English and Chinese).

Bakken 1989:
> Børge Bakken: *Kunnskap og Moral. Utdanningsreform i dagens Kina* (Knowledge and Moral. Educational Reform in China Today). Department of Sociology, University of Oslo, Report no. 1, Oslo, 1989.

Brown 1982:
> Hubert O. Brown: "Politics and the "Peking Spring" of Educational Studies in China", *Comparative Education Review*, vol. 26, no. 3, 1982, pp. 329-351.

Brugger 1986:
> Bill Brugger: "From "Revisionism" to "Alienation", from "Great Leaps" to "Third Wave", *The China Quarterly*, no. 108, Dec. 1986, pp. 643-651.

Census 1982:
> *Zhongguo 1982 nian renkou pucha 10% chouyang ziliao, dianzi jisuanji huizong* (Ten Percent Sample Survey of the Chinese 1982 Census: A Computerized Selection), Beijing, 1982.

Chan 1985:
> Anita Chan: *Children of Mao. Personality Development and Political Activism in the Red Guard Generation*, The Macmillan Press, London and Basingstoke, 1985.

Cheng 1982:
> Cheng Youxin: "On the Essence of Combining Education with Productive Labor", *Social Sciences in China*, vol. III, no. 2, 1982, pp. 76-96.

Ch'ü 1965:
> T'ung-tsu Ch'ü: *Law and Society in Traditional China*, Mouton, Paris, 1965.

Chou 1959:
> Chou En-lai: *Report on the work of the government: delivered at the First Session of the Second National People's Congress on April 18, 1959*, Foreign Languages Press, Peking, 1959.

Christensen and Delman 1981:
> Peer Møller Christensen and Jørgen Delman: "A Theory of Transitional Society. Mao Zedong and the Shanghai School", *Bulletin of Concerned Asian Scholars*, vol. 13, no. 2, April-June, 1981, pp. 2-15.

Deng 1984:
> *Selected Works of Deng Xiaoping (1975-1982)*, Foreign Languages Press, Beijing, 1984.

Dobson 1977:
> Richard B. Dobson: "Social Status and Inequality in Access to Higher Education in the USSR". In *Karabel and Halsey 1977*, pp. 154-175.

Dore 1976:
> Ronald P. Dore: *The Diploma Disease: Education, Qualification and Development*, Allen and Unwin, London 1976.

Fung 1952:
> Fung Yu-lan: *A History of Chinese Philosophy* (translated by Derk Bodde), Vol. 1, Princeton University Press, Princeton, 1952.

GASAT 1983:
> *Girls and Science and Technology, 2: Contributions to the Second GASAT Conference*, The Inst. of Physics, University of Oslo, Oslo 1983.

Grieder 1981:
> Jerome B. Grieder: *Intellectuals and the State in Modern China: A Narrative History*, The Free Press, New York, 1981

Grubb 1985:
> W. Norton Grubb: "The Convergence of Educational Systems and the Role of Vocationalism", *Comparative Education Review*, vol. 29, no. 4, 1985, pp. 526-548.

Goldman 1981:
> Merle Goldman: *China's Intellectuals. Advice and Dissent*, Harvard University Press, Cambridge, Mass., 1981.

Halsey 1961:
> A.H. Halsey, Jean Floud and C. Arnold Anderson (eds.): *Education, Economy and Society. A Reader In the Sociology of Education*, The Free Press, New York and Collier-Macmillan, London, 1961.

Hansen 1982:
> Erik Jørgen Hansen: *Hvem bryder den sociale arv* (Who Breaks the Social Inheritance), vol. 1, Copenhagen, 1982 (with summary in English).

Harding 1987:

Harry Harding: *China's Second Revolution. Reform after Mao*, The Brooking Institution, Washington D.C., 1987.

Hawkins 1974:

John N. Hawkins: *Mao Tse-Tung and Education. His Thoughts and Teachings*, Linnet Books, Hamden, 1974.

Henze 1983:

Jürgen Henze: *Bildung und Wissenschaft in der Volksrepublik China zu Beginn der actziger Jahre*, Mitteilungen des Institut für Asienskunde Hamburg, 132, Hamburg 1983.

Henze 1987:

Jürgen Henze: "Statistical Documentation in Chinese Education: Where Reality Ends and Myths Begin", *Canadian and International Education*, vol. 16, no. 1, 1987, pp. 198-210.

Ho 1962:

Ho Ping-ti: *The Ladder of Success in Imperial China. Aspects of Social Mobility, 1368-1911*, Columbia University Press, New York, 1962.

Hooper 1985:

Beverley Hooper: "The Youth Problem: Deviations From the Socialist Road". In Graham Young (ed.): *China. Dilemmas of Modernization*, Croom Helm, London, 1985, pp. 199-236.

Hooper 1985a:

Beverley Hooper: *Youth in China*. Penguin Books, Ringwood, Victoria, 1985.

Hu 1984:

C.T. Hu: "The Historical Background: examinations and control in pre-modern China", *Comparative Education*, vol. 20, no. 1, 1984, pp. 7-25.

Hu and Seifman 1976:

Shi Ming Hu and Eli Seifman: *Toward a New World Outlook. A Documentary History of Education in the People's Republic of China, 1949-1976*, AMC Press, New York, 1976.

Huazhong Shifan 1984:

Huazhong Shifan Xueyuan Jiaoyu Xi (Education Department, Central China Normal College): *Jiaoyuxue* (Pedagogics), Renmin Jiaoyu Chubanshe, Beijing, 1984.

Jiaoyubu 1980:

Jiaoyubu Putong Jiaoyu Si (Department of General Education, Ministry of Education): *Zhongxue jiaoyu jingyan xuanbian* (A Selection of Secondary Education Experiences), Beijing, 1980.

Jiaoyu Cidian:
   Jiaoyu Cidian, (Dictionary of Education), Jiangxi Jiaoyu Chubanshe, Nanchang, 1987.
Jiaoyu Da Cishu:
   Jiaoyu Da Cishu (Great Encyclopedia of Education), ed. Tang Yue et.al. Revised Edition by Sun Bangzheng, Taiwan Shangwu Yinshuguan, Taibei, 1974.
Jiaoyu Dashiji:
   Zhongguo Jiaoyu Kexue Yanjiusuo (eds.): *Zhonghua Renmin Gongheguo Jiaoyu Dashiji 1949-1982* (Chronology of Important Events in PRC Education 1949-1982), Jiaoyu Kexue Chubanshe, Beijing 1983.
Jiaoyu Gaige:
   Jiaoyu gaige zhongyao wenxian xuanbian (A Selection of Important Documents on Educational Reform), Renmin Jiaoyu Chubanshe, Beijing 1988.

Karabel and Halsey 1977:
   Jerome Karabel and A.H. Halsey: *Power and Ideology in Education*, Oxford University Press, New York, 1977.
Karabel and Halsey 1977a:
   Jerome Karabel and A.H. Halsey: "Educational Research: A Review and an Interpretation". In: *Karabel and Halsey 1977*, pp. 1-85.
Kelly 1981:
   Allison Kelly (ed.): *The Missing Half: Girls and Science Education*, Manchester University Press, Manchester, 1981.
Kvale 1972:
   Steinar Kvale: *Prüfung und Herrschaft*, Beltz Verlag, Weinheim und Basel, 1972.

Li and White 1988:
   Li Cheng and Lynn White; "The Thirteenth Central Committee of the Chinese Communist Party. From Mobilizers to Managers", *Asian Survey*, vol. 28, no. 4, April, 1988, pp. 371-399.
Lewin 1987:
   Keith M. Lewin: "Science Education in China: Transformation and Change in the 1980s", *Comparative Education Review*, vol. 31, no. 3, 1987, pp. 419-441.
Löfstedt 1980:
   Jan-Ingvar Löfstedt: *Chinese Educational Policy*, Almqvist and Wiksell International, Stockholm, 1980.

Löfstedt 1987:

Jan-Ingvar Löfstedt: *Practice and Work in Chinese Education. Why, How and How Much*, University of Stockholm, Center for Pacific Asia Studies, Working Papers 5, Stockholm, 1987.

Mao 1967:

Selected Works of Mao Tse-tung Vol. I-IV, Foreign Languages Press, Peking, 1967-1969.

Mao 1971:

Selected Readings From the Works of Mao Tsetung, Foreign Languages Press, Peking, 1971.

Menzel 1963:

Johanna M. Menzel: *The Chinese Civil Service: Career Open to Talent?*, D.C. Heath and Co., Boston, 1963.

Meyer 1988:

Jeffrey F. Meyer: "Moral Education in Taiwan", *Comparative Education Review*, vol. 32, no. 1, 1988, pp. 20-38.

Miyazaki 1976:

Ichisada Miyazaki: *China's Examination Hell. The Civil Service Examination of Imperial China*, Weatherhill, New York and Tokyo, 1976.

Münch und Risler 1987:

Joachim Münch and Matthias Risler: *Vocational Training in the People's Republic of China. Structures, Problems and Recommendations*, CEDEFOP, Berlin, 1987.

Nathan 1986:

Andrew J. Nathan: *Chinese Democracy*, Tauris, London, 1986.

Parkin 1971:

Frank Parkin: *Class Inequality and Social Order*, London, 1971.

Pepper 1984:

Suzanne Pepper: *China's Universities. Post-Mao Enrollment Policies and Their Impact on the Structure of Secondary Education. A Research Report*, Center for Chinese Studies, The University of Michigan, Ann Arbor, 1984.

Price 1977:

R.F. Price: *Marx and Education in Russia and China*, Croom Helm, London, 1977.

Price 1979:

R.F. Price: *Education In Modern China*, Routledge and Kegan Paul, London, 1979.

Quanguo Zhongxiaoxue 1982:

Quanguo zhongxiaoxue qingong jianxue jingyan xuanbian (Selected National Experiences With Diligent and Frugal Work and Study in Primary and Secondary Schools), Jiaoyu Kexue Chubanshe, Beijing 1982.

Quanguo Zhiye 1986:

Guojia Jiaoyu Weiyuanhui Zhiye Jishu Jiaoyu Si (The Department of Technical and Vocational Education, State Education Commission): *Quanguo zhiye jishu jiaoyu gongzuo huiyi wenjian huibian* (Documents From the National Work Conference On Technical and Vocational Education), Beijing Shifan Daxue Chubanshe, Beijing 1986.

Rawski 1979:

Evelyn S. Rawski: *Education and Popular Literacy in Ch'ing China*, Michigan University Press, Ann Arbor, 1979.

Resolution on CPC History:

Resolution on CPC History (1949-81), Foreign Languages Press, Beijing 1981.

Ridley et al. 1971:

Charles Ridley, Paul Godwin and Dennis Doolin: *The Making of a Model Citizen in China*, The Hoover Institution Press, Stanford, 1971.

Risler 1989:

Matthias Risler: *Berufsbildung in China. Rot und Experte*. Mitteilungen des Institut fur Asienkunde Hamburg, Nr. 179, Hamburg 1989.

Robinson 1986:

Jean C. Robinson: "Decentralization, Money and Power: The Case of People-run Schools in China", *Comparative Education Review*, vol. 30, no. 1, 1986, pp. 73-88.

Rosen 1984:

Stanley Rosen: "New Directions in Secondary Education". In: Ruth Hayhoe (ed.): *Contemporary Chinese Education*, M.E. Sharpe, Armonk, New York, 1984, pp. 65-92.

Rosen 1985:

Stanley Rosen: "Recentralization, Decentralization and Rationalization: Deng Xiaoping's Bifurcated Educational Policy", *Modern China*, vol. 11, no. 3, July, 1985, pp. 301-346.

Rosen 1987:

Stanley Rosen: "Restoring Key Secondary Schools In Post-Mao China: The Politics of Competition and Educational Quality". In: David M. Lampton (ed.): *Policy Implementation in Post-Mao China*, University of California Press, Berkeley, Los Angeles and London, 1987.

Rosen 1987a:

Stanley Rosen: "Survey Research in the People's Republic of China: Some Methodological Problems", *Canadian and International Education*, vol. 16, no. 1, 1987, pp. 190-197.

Schram 1984:

Stuart R. Schram: *Ideology and Policy in China Since the Third Plenum, 1978-84*, Contemporary China Institute, SOAS, London, 1984.

Schram 1987:

Stuart R. Schram: "Ideology and Policy in the Era of Reform, 1976-1986", *Copenhagen Papers in East and Southeast Asian Studies*, no. 1, 1987, pp. 7-30.

Selden 1971:

Mark Selden: *The Yenan Way in Revolutionary China*, Harvard University Press, Cambridge, Mass., 1971.

Seybolt 1973:

Peter J. Seybolt (ed.): *Revolutionary Education in China. Documents and Commentary*, International Arts and Science Press, White Plains, New York, 1973.

Shanghai Shi 1983:

Shanghai shi zhongxue jiaoyu gongzuo xuanbian (A Selection of Experiences from Educational Work in Shanghai Middle Schools), Shanghai, 1983.

Shirk 1973:

Susan Shirk: "The 1963 Temporary Work Regulations for Full-time Middle and Primary Schools: Commentary and Translation." *The China Quarterly*, no. 55, July-September 1973, pp. 511-546.

Shirk 1982:

Susan L. Shirk: *Competitive Comrades. Career Incentives and Student Strategies in China*, University of California Press, Berkeley and Los Angeles, 1982.

Statistical Yearbook of China 1983, 1984, 1985, 1986:

Statistical Yearbook of China 1983, 1984, 1985, 1986. Compiled by the State Statistical Bureau, PRC. Published by Economic Information & Agency, Hong Kong, 1983, 1984, 1985, 1986.

Sullivan 1985:

Michael Sullivan: "The Ideology of the Chinese Communist Party Since the Third Plenum." In: Bill Brugger (ed.): *Chinese Marxism in Flux 1978-84. Essays on Epistemology, Ideology and Political Economy*, Croom Helm, London, 1985, pp. 67-97.

Ten Great Years:
> *Ten Great Years. Statistics of Economic and Cultural Achievements of the People's Republic of China.* Compiled by the State Statistical Bureau. Foreign Languages Press, Peking 1960.

Thøgersen 1987:
> Stig Thøgersen: "China's Senior Middle Schools in a Social Perspective: A Survey of Yantai District, Shandong Province", *The China Quarterly*, no. 109, March 1987, pp. 72-100.

Thøgersen 1989:
> Stig Thøgersen: "Through the Sheeps Intestines - Selection and Elitism in Chinese Schools", *The Australian Journal of Chinese Affairs*, no. 21, Jan. 1989, pp. 29-56.

Unger 1982:
> Jonathan Unger: *Education Under Mao. Class and Competition in Canton Schools, 1960-1980*, Columbia University Press, New York, 1982.

Wang 1966:
> Y.C. Wang: *Chinese Intellectuals and the West, 1872-1949*, The University of North Carolina Press, Chapel Hill, 1966.

Wang 1975:
> Wang Hsueh-wen: *Chinese Communist Education: The Yenan Period*, Institute of International Relations, Taipei, 1975.

White 1981:
> "Higher Education and Social Redistribution in a Socialist Society: The Chinese Case", *World Development*, vol. 9, 1981, pp. 149-166.

Wilson 1970:
> Richard Wilson: *Learning to be Chinese. Political Socialization of Children in Taiwan*, MIT Press, Cambridge, Mass., 1970.

World Bank 1985:
> The World Bank: *China: Long-Term Issues and Options. Annex A: Issues and Prospects in Education*, The World Bank, 1985.

World Bank 1987:
> The World Bank: Sector Report: *Technical/Vocational Education for China's Development*, The World Bank, 1987.

Wu and Zhang 1981:
> Wu Fan and Zhang Hao: "Jiaoyu jiegou he jiaoyu tizhi" (The Structure of Education and the Educational System). In Ma Hong and Sun Shangqing (eds.): *Zhongguo jingji jiegou gaige wenti yanjiu* (Research on Problems in the Reform of China's Economic Structure), vol. 2, pp. 625-652, Renmin Chubanshe, Beijing, 1981.

Ye 1985:
> Ye Yiduo (ed.): *Nan nü sheng de xuexi xinli chayi* (Psychological Differences Between Boys and Girls in Regard to Their Studies), Fujian Jiaoyu Chubanshe, Fujian, 1985.

Zhongguo Baike Nianjian 1982, 1988:
> *Zhongguo Baike Nianjian 1982, 1988* (Encyclopedic Yearbook of China 1982, 1988), Zhongguo Da Baike Quanshu Chubanshe, Shanghai and Beijing, 1982, 1988.

Zhongguo Jiaoyu Nianjian 1949-1981:
> Zhongguo Jiaoyu Nianjian Bianjibu (eds.): *Zhongguo Jiaoyu Nianjian (1949-1981)* (China Education Yearbook 1949-1981), Zhongguo Da Baike Quanshu Chubanshe, Beijing 1984.

Zhongguo Jiaoyu Nianjian 1982-1984:
> Zhongguo Jiaoyu Nianjian Bianjibu: *Zhongguo Jiaoyu Nianjian 1982-1984* (China Education Yearbook 1982-1984), Hunan Jiaoyu Chubanshe, Changsha, 1986.

Zhongguo Jiaoyu Tongji Nianjian 1987:
> Guojia Jiaoyu Weiyuanhui Jihua Caiwu Ju (eds.): *Zhongguo Jiaoyu Tongji Nianjian 1987* (Statistical Yearbook of Chinese Education 1987), Beijing Gongye Daxue Chubanshe, Beijing, 1988.

Zhongguo Jingji Nianjian 1983:
> *Zhongguo Jingji Nianjian 1983* (Yearbook of China's Economy 1983), Xianggang Zhongguo Jingji Nianjian Youxian Gongsi, Beijing and Hong Kong, 1983.

Zhongguo Tongji Nianjian 1988, 1989:
> Zhongguo Tongji Ju (eds.): *Zhongguo Tongji Nianjian 1988, 1989* (Statistical Yearbook of China 1988, 1989) Zhongguo Tongji Chubanshe, Beijing, 1988, 1989.

Tables

Table 2.1:
Number of General Senior Secondary School Graduates and University Enrolment 1949-1988

Year	Secondary school graduates (1,000s)	University enrolment (1,000s)	Secondary school graduates per university enrollee
1949	61.4	30.6	2.01
1950	62.2	58.3	1.07
1951	58.8	51.7	1.14
1952	36.0	78.9	0.46
1953	56.2	81.5	0.69
1954	67.9	92.3	0.74
1955	99.0	97.8	1.01
1956	153.6	184.6	0.83
1957	187.1	105.6	1.77
1958	197.4	265.6	0.74
1959	299.7	274.1	1.09
1960	288.3	323.2	0.89
1961	379.4	169.0	2.24
1962	411.5	106.8	4.13
1963	433.0	132.8	3.26
1964	366.8	147.0	2.50
1965	360.4	164.2	2.19
1966	280.1		
1967	268.2		
1968	793.8		
1969	380.2		
1970	675.5		
1971	1004.4	42.4	23.69
1972	2159.1	133.6	16.16
1973	3494.4	150.0	23.30
1974	4178.9	165.1	25.31
1975	4470.3	190.8	23.43
1976	5172.2	217.0	23.84
1977	5858.3	273.0	21.46
1978	6826.9	401.5	17.00
1979	7265.4	275.1	26.41

Year	Secondary school graduates (1,000s)	University enrolment (1,000s)	Secondary school graduates per university enrollee
1980	6161.5	281.2	21.91
1981	4861.2	278.8	17.44
1982	3105.7	315.1	9.86
1983	2350.9	390.8	6.02
1984	1898.4	475.2	3.99
1985	1966	619	3.18
1986	2240	572	3.92
1987	2468	617	4.00
1988	2506	670	3.74

Sources:
1949-1984: *Jiaoyu Yanjiu* (Educational Research) no. 3, 1986, p. 11.
1985-88: *Zhongguo Tongji Nianjian 1989*, pp. 798-800.

Table 2.2:
Breakdown of Full-time Teachers in Secondary School
by Level of Education

Year	Total	Completion of normal course in higher education or higher	Incomplete higher education or graduates of short-cycle course	Complete secondary or or lower
Senior section				
1953	20,959	68.8%	17.4%	13.8%
1959	63,085	40.4%	44.7%	14.9%
1963	80,131	59.3%	35.1%	5.6%
1978	741,299	45.9%	7.3%	46.8%
1980	570,692	35.9%	28.8%	35.3%
1983	451,111	40.4%	38.0%	21.6%
1987	543,897	40.1%	47.1%	12.8%
Junior section				
1953	103,739	32.2%	21.3%	46.5%
1959	287,374	7.3%	34.0%	58.7%
1963	340,334	28.3%	46.4%	25.3%
1978	2,440,700	7.6%	2.2%	90.2%
1980	2,449,058	4.2%	8.5%	87.3%
1983	2,145,789	5.5%	18.4%	76.1%
1987	2,326,527	5.3%	27.5%	67.3%

Sources:
Achievement of Education, p. 195
Zhongguo Jiaoyu Tongji Nianjian 1987, pp. 62-63.

Table 5.1
The Structure of China's Educational System
in the 1980s

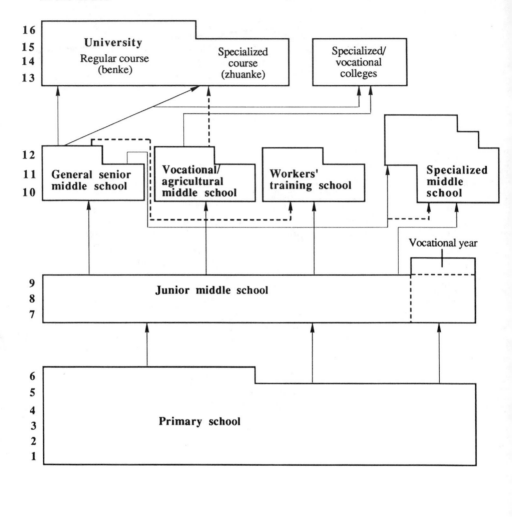

――――――――― desired flow of students

------------- undesired flow of students

Table 5.2
Weekly Lessons in Secondary School According to the 1981 Instruction Plan
(Full-time key schools, six-year course)

Subject	Junior section first year	second year	third year	Senior section first year	second year	third year	Total no. of lessons
Politics	2	2	2	2	2	2	384
Chinese	6	6	6	5	4	4	1,000
Math	5	6	6	5	5	5	1,026
Foreign languages	5	5	5	5	5	4	932
Physics		2	3	4	3	4	500
Chemistry			3	3	3	3	372
History	3	2		3			266
Geography	3	2			2		234
Biology	2	2				2	192
Physiology/Hygiene			2				64
Phys.Ed.	2	2	2	2	2	2	384
Music	1	1	1				100
Art	1	1	1				100
Elective courses					4	4	240
No. of weekly lessons	30	31	34	29	30	30	

Source:
Zhongguo Jiaoyu Nianjian 1949-1981, p. 158

Table 5.3

Government Educational Investments Compared to GNP, National Income and

Financial Expenditures

Figures in billion *yuan*

Year	1977	1978	1979	1980	1981	1982	1983	1984	1985	1986	1987
Educational investments	6.36	7.94	9.59	11.66	12.66	14.18	16.08	19.11	24.10	28.38	30.08
hereof: operating expenses	5.30	6.56	7.70	9.42	10.25	11.57	12.79	14.82	18.42	21.42	22.67
capital construction expenses	0.38	0.65	1.11	1.40	1.51	1.75	2.41	3.16	4.38	5.60	5.91
expenditures of ministeries and commissions on education	0.68	0.73	0.78	0.84	0.90	0.86	0.88	1.13	1.30	1.39	1.49
Supplementary education fees										0.80	1.50

Educ. investments in percent of GNP									2.90	3.03	2.75
Educ. investments in percent of national income	2.58	2.64	2.86	3.16	3.21	3.33	3.44	3.39	3.44	3.64	3.29
Educ. investment in percent of financial expenditures	7.54	7.14	7.53	9.61	11.35	12.30	12.44	12.36	13.06	12.39	12.40

Source:
JYYJ no. 7, 1988, p. 23-36, 31

Note:
Statistics in this field are not always fully reliable.
Slightly diverging figures are found in *WB* 1985, p. 47 and *ZGJYB*, 18 August, 1988, p.4.

Table 6.1:
Number of Students in Secondary School (1,000s)

Year	Number of students in school			Entrants		Graduates	
	junior	general senior	senior, all types	junior	general senior	junior	general senior
1949	832	207		341[1]	71[1]	219[1]	61[1]
1959	7,743	1,436		3,183	656	1,491	299
1962	6,189	1,339		2,383	417	1,584	441
1965	8,030	1,308		2,998	459	1,738	360
1968	12,515	1,403		6,485	630	5,190	794
1971	25,689	5,587	5,814	12,349	3,213	8,350	1,004
1974	26,476	10,027	10,797	13,451	5,411	10,606	4,179
1976	43,529	14,836	15,747	23,443	8,611	12,060	5,172
1977	49,799	18,000	18,932	23,677	9,931	15,586	5,858
1978	49,952	15,531	16,802	20,060	6,929	16,926	6,827
1979	46,130	12,920	14,758	17,278	6,141	16,579	7,265
1980	45,383	9,698	11,960	15,509	3,834	9,648	6,162
1981	41,446	7,150	9,275	14,127	3,278	11,542	4,861
1982	38,880	6,405	8,530	13,631	2,793	10,322	3,106
1983	37,688	6,290	8,876	13,171	2,598	9,603	2,351
1984	38,643	6,898	10,593	13,025	2,623	9,504	1,898
1985	39,648	7,411	11,567	13,494	2,575	9,983	1,966
1986	41,166	7,734	12,526	13,866	2,573	10,570	2,240
1987	41,744	7,737	12,892	13,943	2,552	11,173	2,468
1988	40,155	7,460	13,467	13,405	2,443	11,572	2,506

Sources: 1949-1981: *Zhongguo Jiaoyu Nianjian 1949-1981*, p. 1001
1982-1987: *Zhongguo Tongji Nianjian 1989*, pp. 796-800
Senior, all types, cf. Table 8.1

[1] Figures for 1950.

Table 6.2:
Transition Rates From Primary and Junior Secondary School

Year	Primary school graduates (1,000s)	Junior middle school entrants (1,000s)	Transition rate	Junior middle school graduates (1,000s)	Senior middle school entrants[1] (1,000s)	Transition rate
1952	1,490	1,430	96%	185	312	169%
1957	4,980	2,199	44%	1,112	442	40%
1962	5,590	2,533	45%	1,584	475	30%
1965	6,676	5,507	83%	1,840	1,215	66%
1970	16,525	11,763	71%	6,189	2,390	39%
1975	19,994	18,105	91%	10,476	6,331	60%
1978	22,879	20,060	88%	16,926	6,929	41%
1980	20,533	15,576	76%	9,649	1,161	43%
1983	19,807	13,338	67%	9,603	3,405	36%
1985	19,999	13,670	68%	9,983	3,936	39%
1986	20,161	14,020	70%	10,570	4,000	38%
1987	20,430	14,109	69%	11,284	4,034	36%
1988	19,304	13,372	69%	11,169	4,020	34%

Source:
Zhongguo Jiaoyu Tongji Nianjian 1988, p. 811.

[1]Apparently, this figure includes all junior middle school graduates entering any type of senior middle school, but not general senior middle school graduates entering specialized middle schools or workers' training schools.

Table 6.3:
Distribution of Middle School Students in Urban and Rural Schools (1,000s)

Year	Total number	Urban	%	County seats and towns	%	Rural	%
Senior section - general							
1962	1,339	571	42.6%	664	49.6%	104	7.8%
1965	1,308	564	43.1%	625	47.9%	119	9.0%
1971	5,587	1,269	22.7%	895	16.0%	3,423	61.3%
1977	18,000	3,536	19.6%	2,567	14.3%	11,897	66,1%
1979	12,920	3,511	27.2%	2,602	20.1%	6,807	52.7%
1981	7,150	1,963	27.4%	2,165	30.3%	3,022	42.3%
1983	6,290	1,838	29.2%	2,335	37.1%	2,117	33.7%
1987	7,737	2,269	29.3%	3,425	44.3%	2,043	26.4%
1988	7,460	2,229	29.9%	3,310	44.4%	1,921	25.8%
Junior section							
1962	6,188	2,175	35.2%	1,716	27.7%	2,297	37.1%
1965	8,029	3,381	42.1%	1,945	24.2%	2,703	33.7%
1971	25,689	4,884	19.0%	2,063	8.0%	18,742	73.0%
1977	49,799	7,018	14.1%	4,200	8.4%	38,581	77.5%
1979	46,130	5,809	12.6%	4,432	9.6%	35,889	77.8%
1981	41,446	5,578	13.5%	4,633	11.2%	31,235	75.3%
1983	37,687	5,803	15.4%	5,016	13.3%	26,868	71.3%
1987	41,739	6,064	14.5%	7,129	17.1%	28,550	68.4%
1988	40,155	6,124	15.3%	6,932	17.3%	27,100	67.5%

Sources:
1962-1983: *Achievement of Education,* p. 197
1987: *Zhongguo Tongji Nianjian* 1988, p. 901
1988: *Zhongguo Tongji Nianjian* 1989, p. 823

Table 6.4:
Female Students as a Percentage of All Students

Year	primary school	junior and general senior middle school	agricultural and vocational school	secondary specialized school teachers' training	technical	university
1949	28[1]	27[2]		26[1]	32[1]	20
1959	39	31	23[3]	37	27	23
1962	35	34		49	40	25
1965	40	32	26	49	38	27
1974	44	38			38	34
1976	46	40			36	33
1977	45	42			35	30
1978	45	42		30	35	24
1979	45	41		25	35	24
1980	45	40	33	26	35	23
1981	44	39	40	29	36	24
1982	44	39	39	34	35	27
1983	44	40	39	37	35	27
1984	44	40	41	31		29
1985	45	40	42	30		30
1986	45	41	43	44		26
1987	45	41	44	50	43	33
1988	46	41	44		46	33

[1] Figures for 1951.
[2] Figure for 1950.
[3] Figure for 1958.

Sources:
Zhongguo Jiaoyu Nianjian 1949-1081, p. 1017
Zhongguo Jiaoyu Tongji Nianjian 1987, p. 20
Achievement of Education, p. 40
Statistical Yearbook of China 1985, p. 588
Statistical Yearbook of China 1986, p. 640
Zhongguo Tongji Nianjian 1989, p. 813

Table 6.5:
Completion Ratio in Junior Middle School (estimate) (1,000s)

Intake (year)		Graduates (year)		Completion ratio
1962:	2,383	1965:	1,738	73%
1975:	18,105	1978:	16,926	93%
1976:	23,443	1979:	16,579	71%
1977:	23,677	1980:	9,648	41%
1978:	20,060	1981:	11,542	58%
1979:	17,278	1982:	10,322	60%
1980:	15,509	1983:	9,603	62%
1981:	14,127	1984:	9,504	67%
1982:	13,631	1985:	9,983	73%
1983:	13,171	1986:	10,570	80%
1984:	13,025	1987:	11,173	86%
1985:	13,494	1988:	11,572	86%

Sources:
Zhongguo Tongji Nianjian 1989, pp. 798-800.

Table 8.1:
Number of Students in Various Types of Senior Secondary School
(1,000s)

Year	Total	General schools	Agri-cultural[1]	Voca-tional[1]	Secondary specialized[2]: Teach. Training	Tech-nical	Workers' training school	4 vocational streams in percent of total
1971	5,814	5,587			120	98	9	4%
1974	10,797	10,027			285	349	136	7%
1976	15,747	14,836			304	386	221	6%
1977	18,932	18,000			298	391	243	5%
1978	16,802	15,531			360	529	382	8%
1979	14,758	12,920			484	714	640	12%
1980	11,960	9,698	193	126	482	761	700	19%
1981	9,275	7,150	168	209	437	632	679	23%
1982	8,530	6,405	229	345	411	628	312[3]	25%
1983	8,876	6,290	406	512	455	688	525	29%
1984	10,593	6,898	907	838	511	811	628	35%
1985	11,567	7,411		1,843	562	1,009	742	36%
1986	12,526	7,734		2,143	611	1,146	892	38%
1987	12,892	7,737		2,250	651	1,223	1,031	40%
1988	13,467	7,460		2,794	681	1,368	1,161	45%

Sources:
Zhongguo Jiaoyu Nianjian 1949-1981, pp. 188, 982-83
Zhongguo Jiaoyu Nianjian 1982-1984, p. 95
Zhongguo Tongji Nianjian 1989, pp. 796-97, 810
Achievement of Education, pp. 149, 208-209
Zhongguo Jiaoyu Tongji Nianjian 1987, p. 18.

[1] Includes only students in the senior section, except figure for 1984 which includes some junior middle school students.
[2] Some students in these schools are at the post-secondary level.
[3] Sources for 1981 and 1982 are not identical, which may explain the drop in enrolment.

Table 8.2:
Percentage Distribution of Students in Specialized Middle School by Field of Study

	Technical (total)	Industry	Agriculture	Forestry	Health	Finance and economy	Politics and law	Physical Cult.	Art	Others	Teacher
1949	33.7	9.3	8.9	0.6	6.7	6.5	-	-	-	1.7	66.3
1959	63.9	34.8	13.1	1.8	10.7	0.9	-	0.7	1.1	0.4	36.1
1962	65.9	35.1	8.8	1.2	14.4	3.4	-	0.3	1.9	0.9	34.1
1965	71.7	32.4	8.5	1.4	16.2	10.4	-	0.1	2.1	0.6	28.3
1971	45.0	12.3	5.9		17.3	-	-	-	-	9.5	55.0
1974	55.0	19.9	7.4		19.5	6.1	-	0.4	1.1	0.6	45.0
1976	56.0	17.0	10.0		20.0	6.7	-	0.4	1.2	0.7	44.0
1977	56.7	17.5	10.4		19.3	7.3	-	0.3	1.4	0.5	43.3
1978	59.5	20.4	9.7		17.8	8.5	-	0.4	1.4	1.3	40.5
1979	59.6	20.3	9.2	0.9	17.6	8.8	-	0.4	1.1	1.3	40.4
1980	61.2	21.2	9.1	0.9	18.1	8.6	-	0.5	1.3	1.5	38.8
1981	59.1	19.2	7.8	1.0	17.1	10.0	1.6	0.6	1.5	0.5	40.9
1982	60.4	20.8	7.4	1.2	15.7	10.6	2.1	0.7	1.5	0.4	39.6
1983	60.2	20.5	6.8	1.2	14.3	12.7	2.4	0.6	1.5	0.2	39.8
1984	61.3	20.8	6.5	1.2	13.8	13.8	2.7	0.6	1.5	0.5	38.7
1985	64.2	21.5	6.3	1.2	14.0	15.5	3.1	0.7	1.5	0.4	35.8
1986	65.2	22.2	6.1	1.6	14.0	15.0	2.8	0.8	1.5	1.2	34.8
1987	65.2	21.7	5.6	1.2	14.7	15.7	2.5	1.0	1.5	1.3	34.8
1988	66.7	22.5	5.6	1.2	14.6	16.5	2.2	1.2	1.5	1.3	33.3

Sources:

Achievement of Education, p. 162
Zhongguo Tongji Nianjian 1989, p. 806

Table 10.1:
Education Indicators, 1983

	Yantai [1]	China
Enrolment Rate, Primary Education	98%	94%[2]
Completion Rate[3], Primary Education	98%	60-70%[4]
Graduation Rate[3], Primary Education	91%	30%[4]
Transition Rate, Primary to Junior Secondary	85+%	67%[5]
Transition Rate, Junior to Senior Secondary	24%	36%[5]
Transition Rate, General Senior Secondary to University	36%	17%[6]

[1]   Source: Yantai Educational Bureau.
[2]   *Achievement of Education,* p 15
[3]   The completion rate indicates how many school starters finished five or six years of primary schooling, while the graduation rate indicates the proportion of school starters who graduated with satisfactory results.
[4]   There is no precise information on national completion and graduation rates, but 60-70% and 30% were the figures normally given by Chinese education authorities in the early 1980s.
[5]   of. Table 6.2.
[6]   cf. Table 2.1.

Table 10.2:
Senior Middle Schools and Students in Yantai, 1980-1984[1].

	1980[2]	1982[2]	1984[3]
General Schools	390	130	103
Students	93,839	53,582	55,375
Vocational Schools		80	137[4]
Students	4,421	16,617	20,488[4]
Total: Schools		210	240
Students	98,260	70,199	75,863
Vocational in percent of total	4.5%	23.7%	27%

[1] For comparable national figures see *Statistical Yearbook of China 1983*, p. 512, and *Statistical Yearbook of China 1984*, p. 488.
JYYJ, no. 11, 1983, pp. 20-24.
[2] Source: Yantai Educational Bureau.
[3] Only schools enrolling junior middle school graduates are included in 1984 figures (cf. Table 10.3), 1982 figures probably also include specialized middle schools, which enroll senior middle school graduates.

Table 10.3:
Vocational Education in Yantai, Spring 1984

	Schools	*Students*
Vocational Schools	2	1,314
Vocational Classes[1]	30	
Agricultural Technical Schools[2]	38	5,786
Agricultural Middle Schools	75	5,475
Workers' Training Schools	10	2,257
Teachers' Training Schools	7	3,690
Specialized Middle Schools[3]		
Industry	5	1,953
Agriculture	2	658
Health	4	1,790
Accountancy	1	382
Art	1	176
Subtotal	13	4,959
Total	145	23,481

Source:
Yantai Educational Bureau.

[1] These classes are set up in general schools, but follow a vocational school curriculum. They are not included in the total number of schools below. Their students are included in the 1,314 vocational school students.

[2] Agricultural technical schools are run by the counties and are normally of a higher standard than agricultural middle schools run by lower levels.

[3] Schools in industry, agriculture and accountancy enrolled only senior middle school graduates, while health and art schools accepted junior middle school graduates. The former group of schools is therefore not included in the 1984 figures in Table 10.2.

Table 10.4:
Number of Students and Teachers in Six Yantai Schools.

	Students	Classes	Teachers[1]	Students per class	Students per teacher
City Key	2,074	36	111	58	19
City Non-key	1,806	32	111	56	16
City Vocational	1,483	30	81	49	18
County Key	1,065	19	78	56	14
Agricultural	302	6	29	50	10
Teachers' Tr.	769	16	73	48	11

Source:
Interviews at the six schools.

[1] Staff with non-teaching functions not included.

Table 10.5:
Teachers by Level of Education

Teachers' Educational Background	City Key (N=111)	City Non-key (N=111)	City Vocational (N=8_)	County Key (N=78)	Agricultural (N=29)	Teachers' Training (N=73)
University	76%	54%	60%	76%	52%	81%
Senior Secondary	24%	41%	20%	25%	47%	19%
Junior Secondary or Less	-	5%	2%	-	-	-
No Information	1%	-	17%	-	-	-

Source: Interviews at the six schools.

Table 10.6:
Students' Occupation After Graduation, 1983

1983 Graduates Occupation	City Key (N=290)	City Non-key (two voca tional classes) (N=101)	City Vocational (N=123)	County Key (N=446)	Agricultural (N=88)	Teachers' Training (N=?)
University	37%	-	7%	50%	-	-
Other Further Education	3%	-	-	11%	6%	-
White Collar, Teacher, etc.	15%	-	2%	2%	35%	100%
Worker	24%	97%	89%	3%	19%	-
Peasant	-	-	-	7%	28%	-
Soldier	4%	2%	2%	1%	11%	-
Other or No Occupation	18%	1%	-	26%	-	-

Source: Interviews at the six schools.

Table 10.7:
Occupation of Students' Fathers, Urban Schools

Fathers' Occupation	City Key (N=89)	City Non-key (N=104)	City Vocational (N=98)	National Male City Workforce, Age 35-39 (estimate)[2]	Same, Excluding Peasants
Cadre	42%	43%	29%	20%	24%
Intellectual	19%	17%	17%	13%	16%
Non-manual worker	15%	14%	14%	10%	13%
Manual worker	20%	20%	37%	38%	47%
Peasant[3]	2%	3%	-	20%	-
Others	-	2%	2%	-	-

Source: Questionnaire survey.

[1] For a definition of occupational categories see note 20. p. 142
[2] Figures for the national workforce are calculated from *Census 1982*, Table 35, corrected for age (Table 38). Cadres fall into groups 2 and 3 in Table 35 ("responsible people in state organs, party and mass organizations and enterprises" and "administrative technicians"), non-manual workers into groups 4 and 5 ("commercial personnel" and "service personnel"), workers into group 7 ("productive workers, transport workers and related personnel") and peasants into group 8 ("workers in agriculture, forestry, animal husbandry and fishery").
[3] Peasant children are not allowed to enrol in urban vocational schools.

Table 10.8
Education of Students' Fathers, Urban Schools

Father's Education	City Key (N=88)	City Non-key (N=103)	City Vocational (N=92)	National Non-peasant Male Workforce, Age 35-39 (estimate)[1]
University	16%	17%	18%	9%
Senior or Specialized Secondary	34%	28%	24%	18%
Junior Secondary	36%	38%	34%	34%
Primary	11%	18%	22%	33%
Illiterate	3%	-	2%	6%

Source: Questionnaire survey.

[1] Based on *Census 1982*, Table 40 (excluding peasants), corrected for age (Tables 26, 28 and 29) and sex (Tables 5 and 25). "Non-peasant" and "city" workforces are, of course, not identical concepts, but as close as we can get from the census figures published up to now.

Table 10.9:
Monthly Income of Students' Fathers, Urban Schools

Father's Income	City Key (N=83)	City Non-key (N=100)	City Vocational (N=93)
Less than 50 *yuan*	1%	-	1%
50-70 *yuan*	27%	13%	17%
70-90 *yuan*	55%	47%	46%
more than 90 *yuan*	17%	40%	35%

Source: Questionnaire survey.

Table 10.10:
Occupation of Students' Fathers, Rural Schools

	County Key (N=108)	Teachers' Training (N=98)	Agricultural (N=86)	National Male Rural Workforce Age 35-39 (estimate)[1]
Cadre	15%	15%	7%	5%
Intellectual	11%	13%	6%	6%
Non-manual Worker	12%	5%	2%	4%
Manual Worker	14%	11%	8%	10%
Peasant	49%	53%	77%	74%
Others	-	2%	-	-

Source: Questionnaire survey.
[1] Calculated along the lines of Table 10.7. The rural workforce is counted as the "town" (*zhen*) and "county" (*xian*) workforce in Table 35 of *Census 1982*.

Table 10.11:
Education of Students' Fathers, Rural Schools

Fathers' Education	County Key (N=108)	Teachers' Training (N=96)	Agricultural (N=85)	Male Shandong Population, Age 35-39 (estimate)[1]
University	6%	2%	1%	1%
Specialized Middle School	4%	8%	5%	-
Senior Secondary	22%	19%	14%	6%
Junior Secondary	48%	44%	51%	20%
Primary	20%	22%	24%	47%
Illiterate	0%	4%	3%	26%

Source: Questionnaire survey.
[1] From *Census 1982*, Tables 5 and 25, corrected for age (Table 26).

Table 10.12:
Students' Academic Performance and Fathers' Education:
Three General Schools

Fathers' Education	Combined Examination Score in 5 subjects: Less than 360	360-400	More than 400
University (N=63)	27%	25%	47%
Senior Secondary (N=28)	32%	32%	35%
Junior Secondary (N=78)	20%	32%	48%
Primary (N=28)	18%	35%	47%

Source: Questionnaire survey.

Table 10.13:
Students' Academic Performance and Fathers' Occupation:
Three General Schools

| Fathers' Occupation | Combined Examination Score in 5 subjects: | | |
	Less than 360	360-400	More than 400
Cadre (N=80)	32%	28%	40%
Intellectual (N=36)	22%	19%	58%
Non-manual Worker (N=27)	18%	33%	49%
Manual Worker (N=39)	21%	36%	44%

Source: Questionnaire survey.

Table 10.14:
Students' Career Plans and Fathers' Occupations: Three General Schools

Students' Plans[1]

Fathers' Occupation	Go to University	Go to Specialized Middle School	Non-manual Worker	Manual Worker	Peasant	Join the PLA[2]
Cadre	61%	10%	2%	8%	0%	18%
Intellectual	72%	2%	2%	11%	0%	4%
Non-manual Worker	67%	5%	2%	5%	2%	14%
Manual Worker	72%	6%	7%	2%	4%	13%

Source:
Questionnaire survey

[1] Some students gave more than one answer
[2] PLA = People's Liberation Army

Table 10.15:
Girls as a Percentage of All Students

	Urban	*Rural*
City Key	49%	
City Non-key	48%	
City Vocational	65%	
County Key		43%
Teachers' Training		31%
Agricultural		33%

Source: Interviews at the six schools.

Table 10.16:
Girls as a Percentage of All Students,
City Vocational School

Specialization	*Girls*
Kindergarden Teachers	100%
Accountants	85%
Clock-factory Workers	68%
Artists	56%
Brewery Workers	53%
Engine Fitters	48%
Metal Workers	30%

Source: Interview at Yantai No. 1 Vocational Middle School.

Table 10.17:
Girls in Urban and Rural Schools According to Fathers' Occupation

Fathers' Occupation	Girls in Percentage of All Students Urban	Rural
Cadre	54%	54%
Intellectual	48%	31%
Non-manual Worker	65%	–
Manual Worker	73%	42%
Peasant	–	37%

Source: Questionnaire survey.

Table 10.18:
Boys' and Girls' Academic Performance:
Three General Schools

	Score in 5 Subjects: Less than 360	360-400	More than 400
Boys (N=97)	34%	31%	33%
Girls (N=103)	15%	30%	56%

Source: Questionnaire survey.

Titles of related interest

Rudi Thomsen
Ambition and Confucianism. A biography of Wang Mang
249 pages, paperback. 1988.

Knud Lundbæk
The Traditional History of the Chinese Script
from a Seventeenth-Century Chinese Manuscript
Facismile edition with translation and commentary.
64 pages, hardbound. 1988.

Southeast Asia Between Autocracy and Democracy
Edited by Mikael Gravers et al.
264 pages, paperback. 1989.

AARHUS UNIVERSITY PRESS
Building 170, Aarhus University
DK-8000 Aarhus C, Denmark